D0856262

Rock and Roll Legends

Other Books in the History Makers Series:

America's Founders
Artists of the Renaissance
Astronauts
Cartoonists
Civil War Generals of the Confederacy
Civil War Generals of the Union
Cult Leaders
Dictators
Disease Detectives
Fighters Against American Slavery
Gangsters
Great Authors of Children's Literature
Great Composers
Great Conquerors
Great Male Comedians
Gunfighters
Home Run Kings
Influential First Ladies
Leaders of Ancient Greece
Leaders of Black Civil Rights
Leaders of Women's Suffrage
Magicians and Illusionists
Male Olympic Champions
Native American Chiefs and Warriors
Presidential Assassins
Presidents and Scandals
Rulers of Ancient Egypt
Rulers of Ancient Rome
Scientists of Ancient Greece
Serial Killers
Twentieth-Century American Writers
Women Inventors
Women Leaders of Nations
Women of the American Revolution
Women Olympic Champions
Women Pop Stars

*History*MAKERS

Rock and Roll Legends

By Adam Woog

Lucent Books
P.O. Box 289011, San Diego, CA 92198-9011

On cover: Janis Joplin (upper right); John Lennon (center); Bruce Springsteen (lower left); Jimi Hendrix (lower right).

For Leah, fourth-grader and rock fan

Library of Congress Cataloging-in-Publication Data

Woog, Adam, 1953–
    Rock and roll legends / by Adam Woog.
        p. cm. — (History makers)
    Includes bibliographical references and index.
    Summary: Profiles rock and roll legends including Elvis Presley, John Lennon, Janis Joplin, Jimi Hendrix, Bruce Springsteen, Johnny Rotten, and Kurt Cobain. Also included is a brief history of rock and roll.
    ISBN 1-56006-741-1 (hardback : alk. pap.)
    1. Rock musicians—Biography—Juvenile literature. [1. Musicians. 2. Rock music.] I. Title: Rock and roll legends. II. Title. III. Series.
    ML3929 .W66 2001
    781.66'092'2—dc21
                                    00-011272

Printed in the U.S.A.

CONTENTS

FOREWORD

The literary form most often referred to as "multiple biography" was perfected in the first century A.D. by Plutarch, a perceptive and talented moralist and historian who hailed from the small town of Chaeronea in central Greece. His most famous work, *Parallel Lives*, consists of a long series of biographies of noteworthy ancient Greek and Roman statesmen and military leaders. Frequently, Plutarch compares a famous Greek to a famous Roman, pointing out similarities in personality and achievements. These expertly constructed and very readable tracts provided later historians and others, including playwrights like Shakespeare, with priceless information about prominent ancient personages and also inspired new generations of writers to tackle the multiple biography genre.

The Lucent History Makers series proudly carries on the venerable tradition handed down from Plutarch. Each volume in the series consists of a set of five to eight biographies of important and influential historical figures who were linked together by a common factor. In *Rulers of Ancient Rome*, for example, all the figures were generals, consuls, or emperors of either the Roman Republic or Empire; while the subjects of *Fighters Against American Slavery*, though they lived in different places and times, all shared the same goal, namely the eradication of human servitude. Mindful that politicians and military leaders are not (and never have been) the only people who shape the course of history, the editors of the series have also included representatives from a wide range of endeavors, including scientists, artists, writers, philosophers, religious leaders, and sports figures.

Each book is intended to give a range of figures—some well known, others less known; some who made a great impact on history, others who made only a small impact. For instance, by making Columbus's initial voyage possible, Spain's Queen Isabella I, featured in *Women Leaders of Nations*, helped to open up the New World to exploration and exploitation by the European powers. Unarguably, therefore, she made a major contribution to a series of events that had momentous consequences for the entire world. By contrast, Catherine II, the eighteenth-century Russian queen, and Golda Meir, the modern Israeli prime minister, did not play roles of global impact; however, their policies and actions significantly influenced the historical development of both their own countries and their regional neighbors. Regardless of their relative importance in the greater historical scheme, all of the figures chronicled in the History Makers series made contributions to posterity; and their public achievements, as well as what is known about their private lives, are presented and evaluated in light of the most recent scholarship.

In addition, each volume in the series is documented and substantiated by a wide array of primary and secondary source quotations. The primary source quotes enliven the text by presenting eyewitness views of the times and culture in which each history maker lived; while the secondary source quotes, taken from the works of respected modern scholars, offer expert elaboration and/or critical commentary. Each quote is footnoted, demonstrating to the reader exactly where biographers find their information. The footnotes also provide the reader with the means of conducting additional research. Finally, to further guide and illuminate readers, each volume in the series features photographs, two bibliographies, and a comprehensive index.

The History Makers series provides both students engaged in research and more casual readers with informative, enlightening, and entertaining overviews of individuals from a variety of circumstances, professions, and backgrounds. No doubt all of them, whether loved or hated, benevolent or cruel, constructive or destructive, will remain endlessly fascinating to each new generation seeking to identify the forces that shaped their world.

Testing the Boundaries

Rock and roll has been the dominant form of popular music for over fifty years. It permeates popular culture everywhere—not just in America, where rock was born, but all around the world. It is the soundtrack to modern life.

Defining it, however, can be notoriously hard, because rock comes in many styles. It can be dance music with an irresistible beat, or it can be fragile art. It can be disposable junk, or it can be an emotional cry from the soul. It can be light and silly or it can change people's lives. It can be a symbol of angry rebellion against authority, or a protest against social injustices, or just an awful lot of fun.

One thing that has remained constant about rock and roll is that it is constantly evolving and changing. As it has done so, countless outstanding performers have produced rock and roll. These instrumentalists, composers, and singers have added immeasurably to the development of the music, testing its possibilities and pushing its boundaries in new and exciting ways.

Some of these excellent musicians have become larger-than-life figures. They have become *legends*. A legend is a story people tell about something extraordinary and wonderful that has happened in the past, but the word also refers to the larger-than-life people who appear in those stories.

What Makes a Legend?

Defining a rock legend can be as difficult and subjective as defining rock. There are no hard-and-fast rules determining who becomes a legend, or what factors go into choosing a legend, or whether an individual is truly a legend.

One possible definition of a modern legend might involve fame and celebrity. Some observers argue that if someone is world famous, then that person is legendary. Rock stars are celebrities, certainly; they are familiar names even to those who do not follow music closely, and stories are told about their shocking or outrageous behavior. They have become familiar characters in today's popular culture.

Others will argue, however, that a true legend goes beyond simple fame. After all, celebrity can sometimes be nothing more than the willingness to expose one's private life in gossip magazines or on talk shows. This alone does not guarantee legendary status.

To be considered a genuine legend, other qualities must come into play. A legend has the power to genuinely inspire people. A legend does something that captures the collective imagination. A legend must embody the values and dreams of many people and articulate the feelings of his or her peers. A legend can even become the symbol of a generation.

To be considered a true rock legend, someone should also prove the ability to accomplish some important musical goal. Rock legends extend the boundaries of the music in new and exciting ways or create a lasting body of work from which others draw inspiration.

Being a remarkable individual is perhaps also a prerequisite for becoming a legend. Rock legends almost always have forceful or colorful personalities.

In part because of these forceful personalities, rock legends are often admired by the public. Often, but not always, a legendary figure can be reviled as well. Virtually all of the people in this book were disliked, or even feared, by some members of the public at one time or another. For instance, parents of teenagers in the 1950s disliked and feared Elvis Presley; the U.S. government of the 1970s disliked and feared John Lennon; anyone who did not understand punk music disliked and feared Johnny Rotten.

Some parents dislike and fear rock legends like Elvis Presley.

Similarities

The seven people in this book, though they were (or are) all rockers, achieved legendary status for different reasons. Personally, they are very different from one another. Nonetheless, they also share certain similarities. Most grew up poor, or at least working class. Most began their professional lives against great odds, facing significant opposition to their passion for music from their parents or guardians when they were young.

Furthermore, many developed their talents in relatively isolated parts of the world, places like Port Arthur, Texas; Liverpool, England; and Seattle, Washington. They came of age and became musicians far from the music industry centers of New York and Los Angeles. To persevere and prevail in those circumstances required a strong ego, a stubborn nature, and a powerful will to succeed.

Each person in this book also had a common touch, despite the glamour that is famously a part of the rock-and-roll lifestyle. That is, each could relate to many different kinds of people. Each could express his or her feelings easily and directly to those different groups within larger audiences.

Furthermore, surrounding each of the rock legends in this book, at all times, was an aura of potential. In nearly every case, the attitude was a positive one. The feeling was always "Anything is possible."

Paying the Price

Becoming an accomplished musician—much less a world-famous legend—does not come cheap. Sacrifices are necessary and prices must be paid. Unfortunately, one of the prices often paid by rock legends is a premature death. Of the seven individuals in this book, five died tragically young—by murder, suicide, or accidents aggravated by drug abuse.

The premature deaths of these five were not, of course, the only factors in making them enduring legends. Each had already become an accomplished performer and an important figure in music.

However, for those who died young, death has served a strange purpose. An early death cements the legend. It stops time. It ensures that the individual will always remain larger than life, exactly as he or she was at the time of death. Unfortunately, because so many rock legends have died too soon, the concept of "living fast and dying young" is often seen in society as a crucial part of rock mythology. As critic Dave Marsh mournfully writes, "An early, gruesome demise is built into the legend of pop stardom as most of us understand it."[1]

A notable exception to the rock legend myth of personal excess is Bruce Springsteen, who appears to have succeeded in balancing stardom with sanity. Bono, of the band U2, touched on this aspect of Springsteen's character in a speech inducting him into the Rock and Roll Hall of Fame in 1999. Ironically asking, "Rock stars are supposed to make soap operas of their lives, aren't they?" Bono tallied all the things that Springsteen had avoided: "He hasn't done the things most rock stars do. . . . No drug busts, no blood changes in Switzerland. Even more remarkable, no golf! No bad hair period, even in the eighties. No wearing of dresses in videos."[2]

It is a credit to survivors like Springsteen—the ones who did not burn out young—that their stories continue. They prove that being a genuine rock legend does not require a myth-making early death.

CHAPTER 1

A Brief History of Rock

Rock and roll was born in the late 1940s and early '50s. It was a new style of music that mixed the strong, soulful rhythms of blues music with the harmonies and song structures of country music. These styles had previously been more or less separate, with blues primarily for black audiences and country primarily for white. However, the distinctions began to blur as the new style emerged.

In time it would change and mutate into many new forms. In the beginning, however, rock was characterized by a strong beat driven by electric guitars, saxophones, and drums. Out front was a powerful, charismatic singer. The music, whether fast or slow, was played loudly and passionately. Its deliberately raw and unsophisticated sound contrasted sharply with the dominant style of American popular music, which was characterized by ballad singers like Frank Sinatra—that is, singers of the Great American Songbook that many people associate with Broadway-style musicals.

At first no one knew what to call the new music. Some called it "cat music," perhaps because hip people of the times called each other "cats." Others tried variations on "rhythm and blues," a term that was often used regarding black dance music. Eventually, the name rock and roll was coined, and it stuck. Groups of American teenagers adopted rock and roll as their own; it became a symbol of rebellion against their parents' generation.

Parents were generally confused by it, and some found it dangerous or evil; they feared its unspoken messages of defiance and passion. Likewise, few major record labels were willing to take chances with it; early rock records were released on small independent labels. Most adults figured—and hoped—that rock would be just a quick fad.

Then "Crazy Man Crazy," by a relatively minor band, Bill Haley and the Comets, became a national hit recording in 1953. The tide began to turn. Radio did much to speed the process. DJs like Alan Freed in Cleveland, Ohio, and Dewey Phillips in Memphis, Tennessee, broadcast shows that appealed to young audiences. Although the term "rock and roll" had been slang for some time, Freed's show, "Moondog's Rock and Roll Party," is generally credited with having popularized the phrase.

Rock would not have flourished, however, without the affluent audiences created by the emerging teen culture in America after World War II. Thanks to a strong postwar economy, American teens had more leisure time and money than ever before. For the first time in history, this age group formed a pool of consumers controlling billions of disposable dollars. Much of what they bought revolved around music: records, radios, and "hi-fi" sets (stereo was still in the future).

The First Rockers

Three performers stand out as important shapers of early rock's classic sound and style: Little Richard, Fats Domino, and Chuck Berry. Compared to popular singers like Sinatra, they played and sang with wild abandon. Their lyrics often included nonsense syllables that drove parents crazy; the older generation, accustomed to Broadway musical–style songs, was baffled by something like "Tutti Frutti," which opened with: "A womp bomp a loo bomp a lomp bam boom."

The man behind that song, Little Richard, was not rock's most gifted vocalist, but no one had more attitude—a crucial element in the personas of the early rockers. Little Richard's outrageous stage antics and flamboyant wardrobe set the style for countless other performers and helped the singer (born Richard Penniman in Macon, Georgia) sell millions of records.

With their 1953 hit "Crazy Man Crazy," Bill Haley and the Comets helped rock and roll become a national sensation.

New Orleans singer/pianist Antoine "Fats" Domino stood out thanks to a distinctive Creole-accented vocal style combined with jumping arrangements and rolling piano. The combination was gold: the "Fat Man" sold 65 million records in his career, more than any 1950s rock artist besides Elvis Presley.

Many fans and historians consider Chuck Berry the most important and influential of all the early rockers. The St. Louis native's

Thanks to his animated singing and inventive guitar licks, many consider Chuck Berry the most influential of the early rockers.

songs (which include "Maybellene," "Johnny B. Goode," and "Roll Over Beethoven") are models of wit and compact wordplay. His animated singing and inventive guitar licks, meanwhile, virtually defined the sound of classic rock.

These three, and others like them, were so popular by the mid-'50s that rock and roll became big business. Record companies began signing up dozens of performers, some of whom went on to national fame. Among them were Gene Vincent, Buddy Holly, the Everly Brothers, Roy Orbison, Jerry Lee Lewis, Carl Perkins, and, of course, Elvis Presley.

Some of the most important people in the history of rock stayed out of the spotlight. One was Phil Spector, the man many historians consider rock's first boy genius. Spector was a millionaire by age twenty-one thanks to his uncanny ability to write and produce hits like "(And) Then He Kissed Me," "Be My Baby," and "You've Lost that Lovin' Feeling." Sung by a stable of artists including the Righteous Brothers and the Ronettes, these songs were built on Spector's trademark "wall of sound," a lush, orchestral sound built by using multiples of instruments playing together.

Sonny Bono, a Spector assistant before striking out on his own, felt that Spector's secret lay in his ability to use lyrical images and melodies that anyone could relate to. He recalled that Spector worked hard to make his "little symphonies for the kids" universally appealing: "He used to listen over and over to a new song, and he'd say, 'Is it *stupid* enough, Sonny? Is it *stupid* enough?' What he meant was, is it so simple and direct that *anybody* could get it?"[3]

The British Invasion

By the early 1960s, however, rock had already begun to change and grow. Spector and other producers were experimenting with more sophisticated studio methods. They included using full orchestras, multiples of instruments, and experiments in extending or changing song structures. Rock began to grow away from the simple, straightforward music of the early rockers.

It took an invasion from overseas to return rock to its roots. In England a number of bands had long idolized American rockers. One was the Beatles, who became so popular that they launched a wave of near-hysterical idolatry called Beatlemania. In the wake of Beatlemania, America was crazy about anything from England. Concert promoters and record companies scrambled to sign up new British bands, and they flooded the American market in a phenomenon called the British Invasion.

Though many are now forgotten, some Invasion bands proved to have lasting appeal, including the Who and the Kinks. The most

One of the most popular groups in rock history, the Rolling Stones were part of the British Invasion of the 1960s.

famous and long-lived Invasion band of all was the Rolling Stones, bad-boy counterparts to the Beatles' more upbeat personas. According to a remark attributed to writer Tom Wolfe, the Beatles wanted to hold your hand—but the Stones wanted to burn down your town.

The Invasion bands were important in the history and development of rock because they kept alive the basic roots of the music. They remained grounded in a love of early rock at a time when it was beginning to experiment with new styles. Writer Robert Palmer notes that musicians return regularly to rock's roots, maintaining it as "a developing idiom that periodically refreshes itself by drinking from its own deepest wellsprings."[4]

New Freedom

The experiments and changes in rock exploded in the volatile era commonly called the sixties (which actually spanned the late 1960s and the very early 1970s). The music mirrored the political and social upheavals of the times, which were characterized by antiwar protests, the sexual revolution, the women's movement, and experiments in communal living and drugs. Writer Geoffrey Stokes notes that the era opened doors to "a wide range of musical, intellectual, psychedelic, and role-playing experiments."[5]

In keeping with the volatile times, musicians began exploring exciting new paths. Rock became much freer, and almost any influence—from classical symphonies to jazz riffs to Indian ragas—could

16

be thrown into the mix. A variety of "hyphenated" styles, such as jazz rock and folk rock, sprouted up.

Rock musicians began taking the music far more seriously. For decades popular music had been considered nothing more than entertainment or accompaniment for dancing. Now, musicians wanted their work to be considered art.

Audiences also took it seriously. English teachers analyzed lyrics as poetry. Clergy incorporated rock into religious services. Rock criticism was considered serious journalism. So-called underground radio stations emerged, with DJs playing entire albums uninterrupted by commercials. Fans treated new records like holy texts and searched them for hidden meaning.

By now rock thoroughly dominated popular music, and because it flourished, the music industry was willing to underwrite greater expenses in producing it. For instance, the first Beatles album, produced in 1963, took sixteen hours and about $1,500 to create; in contrast, their 1967 *Sgt. Pepper's Lonely Hearts Club Band* required seven hundred hours and nearly $40,000.

Different Styles

Several styles that evolved out of the experimentation of the sixties were particularly important. One was psychedelia. Psychedelic music, crudely put, was an attempt to recreate the experience of a mind-altering drug trip. It was characterized by long solos, spacey feedback and thundering drums, and augmented by light shows. The effect was electrifying; as guitarist Jerry Garcia of the Grateful Dead put it, "Magic is what we do. Music is how we do it."[6]

Another style that blossomed was folk rock. Part acoustic (nonamplified) and part electric, folk rock emphasized serious lyrics that focused on social change. It merged rock with a craze that had occurred earlier in the decade for

Jerry Garcia and the Grateful Dead's brand of music is known as psychedelic rock.

acoustic folk music—that is, old folk songs or songs that sounded like them.

Folk's leading light, Bob Dylan, virtually invented folk rock in 1965 when he took the radical step of performing with an electric band. The move outraged purist folk fans but gained Dylan a huge new audience. Many bands followed his lead, including Buffalo Springfield and the Byrds.

A few years later, both Dylan and the Byrds spearheaded another style that also merged rock with another, earlier style: country music. Country rock was typified by a simple, spare sound and instruments, such as pedal steel guitars, banjos, and mandolins, long associated with traditional country music. The lyrics of its songs often nostalgically spoke about the simpler pleasures of rural life.

Country rock was a sharp departure from the ornate nature of many of the experiments that took place in '60s era rock. Critic Mikal Gilmore notes, "In effect, [Dylan's country rock album] *John Wesley Harding* flattened the visions and ambitions of psychedelia."[7]

Fragmentation

Rock continued to split into such subgroups, and by the mid-1970s had fragmented into many separate styles. When rock started, a single generation had listened to a single style. Within two decades, however, the audience had grown enormous, embracing more than one generation. Older fans wanted to hear what they'd grown up with, but younger listeners demanded new and different sounds.

As a result, many different styles competed to satisfy listeners separated by such factors as age and class. Bands like Fleetwood Mac and solo artists such as Elton John typified this era. Their emphasis was on pristine studio techniques that created glossy records, and their stage shows were theatrical extravaganzas so big that they could be seen even in the vast stadiums where they performed.

Other '70s styles sought different audience segments. Heavy metal bands like Led Zeppelin used skull-crushing volume and flashy solos that emphasized virtuoso technical skills. Art rock, typified by bands like the Moody Blues, merged the pomp of classical music with rock. The twangy country rock of the Byrds, meanwhile, evolved during this period into a mellow, sleek sound epitomized by the Eagles. Still another style, that of the singer/songwriter, was an extension of the folk rock movement of the sixties. Singer/songwriters typically interpreted their own, intensely personal compositions with sparse acoustic accompaniment. Among the most prominent were Paul Simon, Jackson Browne, James Taylor, and Joni Mitchell. Critic Patrick MacDonald, noting how influential Mitchell has been, writes,

"Joni Mitchell . . . is the mother of almost every female singer working today."[8]

In the eyes of many musicians and fans, this increasing fragmentation was not healthy for rock music. To them, it coupled with the music industry's increasing emphasis on commercialism to make '70s rock bland, flabby, and predictable.

Rock had strayed far from its lively, unruly beginnings. Critic Dave Marsh writes that although a few rockers, including Bruce Springsteen, were keeping this lively spirit going, "the spirit of engagement and vitality had disappeared."[9]

From Punk to Grunge

In 1976 the punk revolution, which began as a grassroots underground movement, turned this tired scene upside down. Punk originated nearly simultaneously in New York and London. In New York the Ramones—perhaps the first true punk band—were celebrated for their cartoonish look and ultra-fast, ultra-loud performances. In London the Sex Pistols were notorious for savage music and provocative, politicized lyrics. Dozens of other bands followed their lead.

Punk was typified by a bare-bones sound that hearkened back to the days of early rock. Joey Ramone of the Ramones commented:

The Ramones were just one of the many bands to emerge during the punk revolution of the late 1970s.

"There was no spirit left, no spark, no challenge, no fun, and so many artists had become so full of themselves. We just weren't hearing any music that we liked anymore, so we stripped it back down and put back the passion and energy and emotion."[10]

Another important aspect of punk was its do-it-yourself philosophy, the idea that anyone could get up onstage. The ability to play was considered unnecessary next to a willingness to participate. As an editorial in the magazine *Sniffin' Glue* put it: "This is a chord. This is another. This is a third. *Now form a band.*"[11]

Related to punk was a branch of rock called new wave, which combined punk with a more polished pop sound. In America the Cars and Blondie were among the more conspicuous new wavers; David Byrne, the leader of Talking Heads, merged his own eccentric compositions with world-beat music, with its influences from around the world, to make music that was both adventurous and commercially successful.

In England the impassioned voice of Chrissie Hynde brought her band, the Pretenders, to the forefront of new wave. The appeal of the Police, meanwhile, lay in the brilliantly catchy songs of bassist/singer Sting and his incorporation of reggae rhythms from Jamaica. And Elvis Costello merged the singer/songwriter tradition with an edgy new-wave sensibility.

Punk directly influenced the next important development in rock: grunge. Musically, grunge's sound was rooted in both the anarchic, do-it-yourself blunt assault of punk and the equally loud but more technically proficient sound of 1970s heavy metal. Philosophically, grunge summed up a generation's sense of discontent and rebellion, as earlier punk songs had done for an earlier generation—and as the earliest rock songs had done for yet another.

Evolving

During the 1980s the course of rock was strongly influenced by developments in technology. These technological advances increased the audience by creating new ways to hear and appreciate music. Personal listening devices with headphones are common today, but when the Sony Walkman was introduced to America in 1980, it was a thrilling, almost revolutionary new way to hear music. At last people could listen to cassette tapes through headphones—and carry them around—without disturbing others.

Cassette tapes experienced a sharp surge in sales and gave the music industry a huge boost. Then came the compact disc, introduced in the mid-1980s. Purists complained that a CD's digitized sound was colder and thinner than analog (that is, vinyl). Nonetheless, the convenience, durability, and extended playing time of CDs

Pictured are the original MTV VJs (L to R): Alan Hunter, Nina Blackwood, Mark Goodman, J. J. Jackson, and Martha Quinn. The debut of MTV in 1981 had a profound impact on rock music.

ensured their popularity, and record companies reaped more profits by reissuing old music in new form.

Another profound change in the way that technology affected rock involved the debut in 1981 of Music Television (MTV). Musicians had made promotional films since the 1930s, but MTV took them to a new level. Sales of albums skyrocketed, especially for musicians with visually arresting videos, such as the Eurythmics, Michael Jackson, and Madonna.

At one time radio had been the most important tool for spreading new music. MTV was just as important when it emerged, and, in the same way, new Internet-based technologies are now beginning to make themselves felt. Such new technology is one of the most powerful tools rockers can use to record their music and get it heard by a widespread audience.

As for the music itself: rock has never stopped changing or evolving, even as it incorporates factors such as new technology. One thing that has remained constant is a rockin' sound. Another constant has been a sense of rebellious defiance against authority and the established order. Throughout this fifty-year history of rebellion and rockin' music, many individuals have made important contributions to it. A few of them have risen to the status of rock legends.

CHAPTER 2

Elvis Presley: The King of Rock and Roll

"Man, when I was nine, I couldn't imagine anyone *not* wanting to be Elvis Presley."

—Bruce Springsteen

The lurid aspects of Elvis Presley's life often outshadow his crucial role in American popular music. His story is a classic rags-to-riches tale of a poor boy who eventually succeeds. Famous in his early performing years as a symbol of rebellion, he became even more famous for the lavish but eccentric lifestyle he adopted as his wealth grew.

Despite the attention focused on his personal life, Elvis remains the single most important figure in the birth of rock and roll. He did not invent rock, but he was immensely influential as a performer, synthesizer of styles, and popularizer. Elvis was not the first rocker, but he was the first to bring rock and roll to a widespread mixed-race audience. As his fame grew, he directly inspired a generation of musicians, including Bruce Springsteen and John Lennon, to pick up guitars and rock out. Furthermore, his movies and public appearances fostered a public image that millions of young people found irresistible: he had a combination of sweetness and sexiness, and of dangerous rebellion and boy-next-door vulnerability.

As an American icon, Elvis has stood the test of time. No other performer in history has had a greater impact on worldwide pop culture. Decades after his death, his name, face, and voice are instantly recognized even in distant corners of the globe. His importance as a cultural icon has only grown in the years since his death. For millions of devoted fans, Elvis was, and always will be, the only king of rock and roll.

Tupelo

Elvis Aron Presley was born on January 8, 1935, in a two-room shack in the small farming community of Tupelo, Mississippi. His father, Vernon, worked occasional odd jobs while his mother, Gladys, stayed at home. The family was poor but devoted to church and to one another.

Elvis's twin, Jesse Aron, was stillborn, and Vernon and Gladys Presley treated their only child with special care. They taught him southern manners—all his life he called his elders "sir" and "ma'am"—and instilled in him concepts of familial love and respect. Elvis grew up quiet, polite, and respectful; his fifth-grade teacher called him "sweet, that's the word. And average. Sweet and average."[12]

For his eleventh birthday, Elvis wanted a bicycle, but his parents couldn't afford one. Instead, Gladys bought him a cheap guitar because Elvis loved music. Elvis's first musical training came when his uncle Vester taught him a few basic chords, but the radio was the primary way Elvis heard music.

In those days people relied on the radio and on themselves for musical entertainment. Radio exposed young Elvis to a wide variety of musical styles, paving the way for future experiments in merging different forms. He heard country singers like Hank Williams, pop stars like Bing Crosby, and black jazz musicians like Louis Armstrong.

Church music was even more important than the radio as an early influence. The Presleys sang hymns in church every Sunday, and Elvis was moved by the passionate gospel quartets that sang for their fundamentalist congregation. Church was a refuge from the grimness of daily life; years later Presley recalled, "When I was four or five, all I looked forward to was Sundays, when we all could go to church. This was the only singing training I ever had."[13]

Memphis

In 1948 the Presleys moved to Memphis, Tennessee, in search of a better life. Vernon found a steady job as a truck driver, and Gladys worked occasionally in factories. The family settled in a low-income housing project and Elvis entered high school.

Music continued to be a passion for Elvis. He liked to sit on the steps of his housing project in the warm Tennessee evenings and practice harmony singing with other boys. He also took guitar lessons from the son of his family's minister.

At age eleven, Elvis Presley received his first guitar.

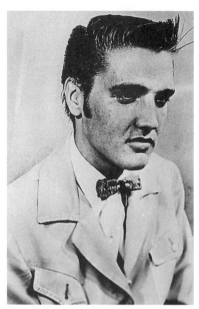

During high school Elvis Presley listened to music from the black community.

Unusual for a white teenager of the times, Elvis was drawn to the music from the black community. He was especially interested in the blues and the dance music called rhythm and blues (R&B), both of which were shockingly sensual styles to most white audiences.

Elvis loved to cruise in his father's Lincoln and listen to a black-owned station, WDIA, where he heard artists like Arthur "Big Boy" Crudup and Wynonie Harris. He attended shows at a black theater and dressed in flashy clothes from a shop that catered to the black community (though his greased-back hair and sideburns were modeled after a style popular with white truck drivers).

After graduating in 1953, Elvis drove a truck for the Crown Electric Company and made his first attempts at singing professionally. He auditioned unsuccessfully for gospel quartets and was so nervous when he tried out for a spot in a local dance band that he failed the audition.

Memphis Recording Service

On a lunch break that summer, Elvis walked into Memphis Recording Service, where $4 let amateur singers make a record of two songs. The studio was owned by Sam Phillips, but his assistant, Marion Keisker, was running the shop that day. She asked Elvis what style he sang. "I sing all kinds," he replied. When Keisker asked, "Who do you sound like?" Elvis replied, "I don't sound like nobody."[14]

Elvis recorded two then-current pop hits, "My Happiness" and "That's When Your Heartaches Begin." Keisker, hearing an unusually dramatic quality in the teen's voice, made an extra copy. She thought Phillips might be interested in Presley for his other business, Sun Records.

Sun was a tiny company that produced early records by such blues and R&B greats as Bobby "Blue" Bland, B. B. King, and Ike Turner. Although Phillips was white, he loved black music with an almost religious fervor. He once remarked, "It seemed to me that the Negroes were the only ones who had any freshness left in their music."[15]

Phillips did not contact Elvis until June 1954, when he asked Elvis to help him with a demo, a rough version of a song used for promotional purposes. The recording session was not a success—Elvis had difficulty getting the tune right—but Phillips was impressed with the breadth of the teen's musical knowledge, ranging from pop to country to blues. Phillips introduced Presley to two working musicians, guitarist Scotty Moore and bassist Bill Black, and encouraged them to regularly rehearse together at Sun.

In early July during a rehearsal break, Presley started fooling around with a song he'd heard on the radio, "That's All Right (Mama)." It had been written and performed by a relatively unknown blues musician, Arthur "Big Boy" Crudup. The others joined in, just goofing around. Phillips, astonished that the kid even knew the obscure song, asked what they were doing. When the musicians replied that they didn't know, he retorted, "Well, back up, try to find a place to start, and do it again."[16]

The Blue Moon Boys

Phillips made the group rehearse incessantly before he recorded the song. Moore recalled how unusual the recording's mix of country and blues sounded: "We thought it was exciting, but what was it? It was just so completely different. But it just really flipped Sam—he felt it really had something."[17]

The record, released in the summer of 1954, was a regional hit, and the trio began appearing at clubs around town as the Blue

Elvis began his rise to stardom as a member of the Blue Moon Boys.

Moon Boys. During their first appearance at a large venue, the open-air Overton Shell, Presley displayed onstage movements that were shocking for the time, shaking and dancing as though he were possessed. He was a sensation: Dewey Phillips, a local disc jockey, recalled that day: "He went into 'That's All Right (Mama)' and started to shake and that damned auditorium just blew apart. He was nobody . . . but the people wouldn't let him leave."[18]

The band also became regular performers on a popular radio show, the *Louisiana Hayride*. Hired to sing every Saturday night, Elvis got $18 per show, while the others received $12. In addition to this windfall, the *Hayride* provided the band with a fourth member; staff drummer D. J. Fontana joined the Blue Moon Boys full-time.

As his regional fame grew, audience response to "the Hillbilly Cat," as Presley was called, became stronger—often positive but sometimes hostile. More than once, Presley had to flee angry young men who thought the singer was exciting their girlfriends a little too much. The first of many Elvis "riots" occurred in Jacksonville, Florida, in May 1955, after the singer joked onstage that he would see all the girls afterward. Backstage, before the band could be hustled away, screaming fans ripped off Presley's jacket, shirt, and shoes.

From the Waist Up

The backstage incident caught the eye of a flamboyant ex-carnival man turned concert promoter, Colonel Tom Parker. The Colonel introduced himself and dazzled Presley with promises of stardom. Elvis resisted signing a management contract with Parker, however, because his parents were still mistrustful of his singing career; in fact, Gladys was hoping that Elvis would settle down and open a furniture shop. By August 1955, however, Parker persuaded the singer to sign an exclusive contract.

The Colonel quickly became the cornerstone of Elvis's career, and from then on Elvis nearly always agreed with his plans even if they resulted in mediocre results. After Presley's death, it was revealed that the Colonel had consistently cheated his client out of millions of dollars. Still, without the Colonel, Elvis would probably never have been more than a regional hit. More than anyone besides the singer himself, Parker made Presley famous.

Word about the hot young singer was getting around the music industry. The Colonel was able to arrange for RCA Records to buy out Elvis's contract with Sun; the $40,000 fee was, at the time, the highest ever paid for a popular entertainer.

Thanks to his new contract with a major label, "Heartbreak Hotel" became Presley's first national hit, in 1956. As hit followed hit, he became the talk of the land. All across the country, Elvis was interviewed by curious reporters; he was always friendly and respectful, calling the reporters "sir" or "ma'am" as he'd been taught.

His career was boosted by appearances on Ed Sullivan's top-rated TV variety show. On the first of these, the charismatic singer was watched by more people than any program in history. After storms of protests about Elvis's gyrating dance steps during his first appearance, Sullivan decreed that the camera would from then on capture Presley from the waist up only. "Elvis the Pelvis," as the press had dubbed him, used the restriction to his advantage: he grinned and wiggled only his shoulders and eyebrows, eliciting as many screams as with his usual routine.

However, Colonel Parker had always seen Presley's career as one that included more than just music. Thanks to a lucrative deal, he was also responsible for Elvis's movie career. Elvis's first film, a Western called *Love Me Tender*, recouped its $1 million expenses in three days. It was followed by *Loving You* and the two that many consider his best, *Jailhouse Rock* and *King Creole*. All were as wildly successful as the first.

Pictured in his army uniform, Elvis Presley departs for military service.

In the Army

Unfortunately, his beloved mother was not able to enjoy Presley's skyrocketing career for long. Her health had been poor for some time; she had long suffered from a weak heart and hepatitis, aggravated by long-term abuse of diet pills and alcohol.

Elvis was one of the most famous people in the country, but he received his draft notice nonetheless and entered the army in 1957. Soon after, Gladys died. Elvis was inconsolable. She and Elvis had always been extremely close, and the singer had rarely been out of her presence for long. "She's all we lived for," he told reporters. "She was always my best girl."[19]

Presley spent his two-year army hitch in Germany, where he served as a Jeep scout. The only special treatment he requested was to live off base, because his father and grandmother had come to live with him. In the army Presley was introduced to two lifelong interests: karate and Priscilla Beaulieu, the fourteen-year-old daughter of an air force officer. He was also introduced to amphetamine, or speed, by fellow soldiers. This was the beginning of a drug habit that would haunt Presley for the rest of his life.

Presley worried that his public would forget him during his army stint. Returning to civilian life in 1959, however, he proved more popular than ever. The album *Elvis Is Back* shot to number one, an appearance on a Frank Sinatra TV special garnered record ratings, and his first post-army film, *G.I. Blues*, was a smash.

Back in Memphis, Elvis invited Priscilla for extended visits to Graceland, the mansion he shared with his father and other family members. With her parents' blessing, she eventually moved into her own suite there. The couple married in April 1967; nine months later, their daughter Lisa Marie was born.

Elvis met his wife Priscilla while stationed with the army in Germany. The couple married in April 1967.

Elvis returned to live performance with his highly successful 1968 Christmas TV special.

A Brief Burst of Energy

After "his boy" returned from the army, the Colonel claimed that touring was no longer profitable enough. He insisted that Elvis concentrate on movies and records, which were cheaply made and always tremendously profitable. Presley's movies routinely made ten times their costs, no matter how mediocre they were or how similar to the last one. Elvis movies were so alike, one film industry executive cracked, that they might as well be numbered.

Throughout most of the '60s, Presley was content to go along with the Colonel's plans, not performing live but annually cranking out two movies and two albums. But he could not resist the challenge laid down by a new musical generation personified by the Beatles and Bob Dylan.

Against the Colonel's wishes, Elvis used a 1968 Christmas TV special for his return to vibrant, live musical performance. Instead of sleepwalking through the mediocre material Colonel Parker preferred, Elvis performed powerful new songs like "Guitar Man." These were better-crafted and tougher-minded songs, unlike the toothless tunes Parker had been pushing (most of which, not concidentally, were published by a company Parker owned).

The show was a triumph. Presley continued its success with extended show dates in Las Vegas and recordings of more superior material. Critics and fans alike cheered Presley's return. It proved that he was far from being a tired has-been. Typical was *Newsweek*'s comment: "There are several incredible things about Elvis, but the most incredible is his staying power in a world where meteoric careers fade like shooting stars."[20]

"Elvis Has Left the Building"

Unfortunately, his renewed energy was short-lived. In large part, this was because Presley's life began to disintegrate. Elvis was either unwilling or unable to escape from his isolation during his many years of stardom. Never able to lead a normal life because of his fame, Elvis was pampered by his entourage, which included three full-time cooks and the so-called Memphis Mafia—a group of friends, bodyguards, and employees that was constantly with him. Elvis began to put on weight and grew increasingly dependent on amphetamines, which he used to keep him alert and try to control his weight.

However, the single biggest factor in Elvis's downhill slide was the failure of his marriage. Priscilla Presley detested Elvis's ever-present entourage of friends, disapproved of how he spoiled Lisa Marie, and worried about his drug use. Early in 1972 she moved to California and filed for divorce. Elvis was stunned. The failure of the marriage sent him into a deep depression and a worsening cycle of drugs and overeating.

His fans continued to worship him, but as his drug use escalated, his work grew indifferent and sloppy. He would drop the microphone onstage, forget lyrics, or ramble incoherently. By the 1970s *L.A. Times* critic Robert Hilburn, once a devoted fan, was moved to write, "Maybe it's time for Elvis to retire. . . . [T]here is no purpose or personal vision in his music anymore."[21]

Presley's health also began to fail; his ailments included hypertension and liver, heart, kidney, colon, and eye problems. Drug abuse and overeating may not have caused these, but they certainly aggravated them.

Offstage he became increasingly eccentric; according to legend, he developed a fondness for shooting television sets when he saw something that displeased him. By their account, friends virtually kept Elvis alive from day to day; one friend, Dave Hebler, remarked, "Sometimes, you think you are looking after a child."[22]

What was destined to be Elvis's last show took place in Indianapolis, Indiana, in the summer of 1977. It ended with the show's standard announcement, designed to discourage fans from trying to get backstage: "Ladies and gentlemen, Elvis has left the building."

People gather outside Graceland following the announcement of Elvis's death.

The Final Rest

On the morning of August 16, 1977, Presley went to bed around 4 A.M. with his new girlfriend, Ginger Alden. Ginger went to sleep while Elvis read in bed. When she awoke that afternoon, Ginger found Elvis in the bathroom. He had suffered a heart attack while reading a book called *The Scientific Search for the Face of Jesus.*

Panicked friends summoned an ambulance. Resuscitation attempts en route and at Baptist Memorial Hospital were of no use. Elvis was dead at the age of forty-two. A hospital executive recalled, "They worked on him for about thirty minutes and then Dr. Nick [Dr. George Nichopolous, Presley's physician] came in, his head down. He said, 'It's over. He's gone.' You could see tears come to his eyes and everybody there started crying."[23]

Within an hour of the announcement, a vigil formed outside Graceland. A crowd estimated at eighty thousand remained for days. Worldwide media covered the event extensively. All the florists in Memphis were sold out. When the public was allowed to view Elvis's body, the line stretched for miles in the ninety-degree heat.

The singer was buried in a nearby cemetery, but after there was an attempt to steal the body, Vernon Presley moved his son to Graceland, where he is buried alongside his mother. Tributes flooded in from around the world. Typical was that of President Jimmy Carter, who reflected that Presley's death "deprives our country of a part of itself," and that his music and personality "permanently changed the face of American popular culture."[24] The king of rock and roll was gone.

CHAPTER 3

John Lennon: Working-class Hero

"The guitar's all very well, John, but you'll never make a living out of it."

—John Lennon's Aunt Mimi

There has never been a band like the Beatles. They raised the bar for every aspect of popular music: racking up dozens of record-breaking hits, setting soaring standards for composition, transforming the art of record production. Beatlemania was the most remarkable cultural and sociological phenomenon of its time; it determined the look, sound, and style of a generation.

Although the Fab Four were a single unit, one figure dominated. John Lennon charmed millions with his personal charisma, quick wit, and fondness for bursting the bubbles of pretentious people. He angered millions with his controversial statements and fierce commitment to political causes. Most of all, as a singer and songwriter, he created some of the most memorable and extraordinary rock ever heard. Lennon and his musical partner Paul McCartney have been likened by many critics to the true greats of music, who created art that was not only popular but has stood the test of time. The enduring popularity of the Beatles among a multi-generational audience lay in the balance of personal styles—McCartney's effortless lightness and Lennon's more somber, serious tone—and the radical mixture of traditional popular music with a wide variety of structures and styles. Even in the years since the band's breakup and his death from an assassin's bullet, Lennon's legend and music remain vital.

Liverpool

John Winston Lennon was born October 9, 1940, in Liverpool, a scruffy port city in northwest England. John's father, Alfred Lennon, abandoned his wife Julia before their son's birth. Julia remarried a man who didn't want children, so John was raised by his Aunt Mimi.

The boy continued to see his mother periodically for years. Many biographers speculate that Lennon's uncertain childhood contributed to the rage and cynicism that later found its way into his music.

An intelligent boy, John was known for his imaginative stories and drawings. But he was also rebellious, leading a gang of wild boys and constantly getting in trouble. He acknowledged that much of his behavior was an attempt to gain attention. By the time he reached Quarry Bank High School, Lennon later recalled, "I wanted to be the leader. . . . I wanted everybody to do what I told them to do, to laugh at my jokes and let me be the boss."[25]

A Band Forms

Making music was a good way to command attention, and leading a band was even better. John pestered Aunt Mimi to buy him a guitar, and in 1955 he formed a band, the Quarrymen, which featured himself on guitar and vocals.

At a church fair where the band was playing for free, Lennon met Paul McCartney. McCartney, only fourteen, impressed the standoffish sixteen-year-old Lennon by revealing talents none of the Quarrymen had: he knew complete song lyrics and could tune a guitar.

Paul became a member of the Quarrymen, and the pair developed an intensely competitive relationship as co-leaders of the band. Though McCartney was the better instrumentalist, they were both good singers and developed a dual-harmony style. They also grew close personally, especially after tragedy struck in 1958. John's mother was killed by a speeding car, and Paul, who had already lost his own mother to cancer, helped John deal with the grief.

As a youth, John Lennon craved attention.

Lennon's first influence was skiffle, a form of British pop combining folk and jazz, and the Quarrymen played a lot of it. But Lennon was also profoundly influenced by American rock, and as his friendship with McCartney (another rock fanatic) developed, the Quarrymen gradually shifted from acoustic skiffle to electrified rock and roll.

The latest American rock was available in Liverpool as in no other British city. The British Broadcasting Company dominated music in England, and it banned rock. But Liverpool, a major port between England and North America, was full of sailors who brought back the latest records. Because of this, Lennon was exposed to rock long before most British teens. He was especially fond of Elvis, as his Aunt Mimi recalled: "I never got a minute's peace. It was Elvis Presley, Elvis Presley, Elvis Presley."[26]

A Hit in England

The band's evolution included several important changes: name changes (settling on the Beatles), the addition of lead guitarist George Harrison, and the replacement of drummer Pete Best with Ringo Starr. The Beatles' mastery of American-style rock—especially "covers," or copies of songs, by American rockers like Chuck Berry or Little Richard—helped them become one of Liverpool's top bands. But a new manager, Brian Epstein, had even bigger plans.

Epstein remade their image. He replaced their tough-guy jeans, leather jackets, and greasy pompadours with stylish suits, new hairstyles, and even classier cigarettes. John, ever the rebel, complained loudly but went along, since Epstein promised it would get them a wider audience.

When they signed a contract in 1962 with Parlophone Records, Lennon and McCartney insisted that the first records be of their own compositions. Their instincts proved right. The first singles caught on

The Beatles (L to R: George Harrison, John Lennon, Pete Best, and Paul McCartney) are pictured just prior to signing their first record contract. Ringo Starr would soon replace Pete Best.

The Beatles' appearance on the Ed Sullivan Show *was the beginning of Beatlemania in the United States.*

immediately in England, and a subsequent LP, filled with the pair's infectious writing and singing, jumped to the top of the charts and stayed for a record-breaking twenty-nine weeks.

Much of what appealed to audiences came from the two songwriting partners. Their temperaments complemented each other and emerged in the songs. John's cheekiness balanced Paul's politeness; Paul's sentimentality checked John's cynicism. Lennon once commented, "He provided a lightness, an optimism, while I would always go for the sadness, the discords, the bluesy notes."[27]

Suddenly Lennon and the rest of the band were headlining shows and encountering mobs everywhere. The British press, disarmed by the band's wit and charm, helped fan the flames of stardom with comments like this one from the *London Daily Mirror:* "You have to be a real sour square not to love the nutty, noisy, happy, handsome Beatles. If they don't sweep your blues away, brother, you're a lost cause."[28]

American Beatlemania

Being stars in England was one thing; conquering America was another. No British act had ever made a dent in U.S. pop charts. The band was stunned, therefore, to learn early in 1964 that their song "I Want to Hold Your Hand" was number one there. Photographer Dezo Hoffman was there when they heard the news. Referring to Lennon's gift for gab, he remarked, "The Beatles couldn't even speak—not even John Lennon."[29]

Their first appearance in America, on the *Ed Sullivan Show,* was so eagerly anticipated by American teens that it became the most-watched entertainment program to date. After that, Beatlemania (as the press dubbed it) spread like wildfire: the band repeatedly smashed sales records, embarked on the most ambitious tours ever made by a pop group to date, and starred in a pair of hit movies.

Within a few years, however, Lennon began to resent being a Beatle. He chafed against the "lovable moptop" image Epstein had created.

Never one to hide his ego or intelligence, Lennon hated it when members of the public spoke down to him. He retaliated with bitter wit. At a fancy party, a woman asked him for an autograph, then turned to a friend and rudely said, "I never thought I would stoop to asking for such an autograph." Lennon remarked, "And I never thought that I would be forced to sign my name for someone like you."[30]

Lennon was always ready to speak his mind, sometimes foolishly but always passionately, on topics that angered or interested him. In 1966 his outspokenness, combined with his astonishment over Beatlemania, created a scandal. A London newspaper quoted the singer expressing wonder that a simple pop band could be so deeply adored that it was as influential as organized religion. "Christianity will go. It will vanish and shrink," he remarked. "[W]e're more popular than Jesus now. I don't know which will go first—rock and roll or Christianity."[31]

The reaction in England to this statement was mild; Britons were accustomed to Lennon making provacative statements. In America, however, the comments were perceived as a boast that the Beatles were "more popular than Jesus." The furor about the out-of-context statement created a huge anti-Beatle backlash. Conservative leaders urged a Beatles boycott, radio stations banned the group, and piles of Beatle records were burned in bonfires.

On a Break

Weary of touring, fighting off crowds, and dodging controversy, the Beatles quit live performance later that year. They spent several months pursuing individual interests before reconvening to create 1967's *Sgt. Pepper's Lonely Hearts Club Band*, the masterpiece many consider rock's first truly important work of art. Although, as usual, Lennon's songs on this landmark album were collaborations with McCartney, Lennon's individuality stood out strongly on such songs as "Being for the Benefit of Mr. Kite!" and the epic "A Day in the Life."

During his time off, Lennon made his first major public appearance alone, playing a supporting role in the film *How I Won the War*. The movie's bitter antiwar message was in tune with the politics of the volatile late '60s. Lennon began making frequent public political statements, especially against the Vietnam War. He also experimented with LSD, pursued an interest in avant-garde art, and studied meditation with a spiritual teacher from India, Maharishi Mahesh Yogi.

All his life Lennon was prone to enthusiasms that quickly came and faded. His interest in the Maharishi was a good example. He accompanied the other Beatles and a number of other celebrities to the guru's compound in India, but soon became disillusioned. According to John, he went to the Maharishi's "very rich-looking bungalow" to announce his departure. When the guru asked why, Lennon replied, "Well, if you're so cosmic, you'll know why." John recalled that "he gave me a look like 'I'll kill you' [and] I knew then . . . I had called his bluff."[32]

"John's in Love with Yoko"

In keeping with his interest in avant-garde art, Lennon in 1966 attended the opening of an exhibit called "Unfinished Paintings and Objects." There he met its creator, Yoko Ono, an American citizen originally from Japan.

Paul McCartney, George Harrison, and John Lennon are pictured with Maharishi Mahesh Yogi. Following the Maharishi was just one of Lennon's many passing interests.

It was the beginning of a passionate romance. Ono's intensity and unconventional ideas fascinated Lennon, and he liked the fact that she, knowing nothing about rock, was unimpressed with his fame. "She encouraged me to be myself," Lennon commented, "because it was me she fell in love with, not the Beatles."[33]

However, Lennon had been married since 1962 to Cynthia Powell, his girlfriend from his early days in Liverpool. The couple had a son, Julian. But the marriage had been stagnant for years, and Cynthia filed for divorce as Lennon's connection with Ono blossomed.

The couple became utterly devoted to one another. The public, meanwhile, was fascinated by the combination of the sarcastic rock star and the mysterious black-clad Ono. During sessions for *The Beatles*, also called the White Album, Ono was a constant presence, even accompanying Lennon to the bathroom. It was the first time anyone besides producer George Martin, engineers, and Beatles employees had been allowed into their tight recording world.

Tensions mounted during the recording. It was becoming clear to the others that Lennon's energy was shifting away from the band. McCartney poignantly commented, "John's in love with Yoko, and he's no longer in love with the three of us."[34]

The Divorce

Lennon and Ono began making increasingly provocative public statements and art on their own, away from the collective grouping of the Beatles. They released an album that featured a scandalous nude cover photo. When they wed in 1969, the honeymoon was spent at the Amsterdam Hilton in a "bed-in for peace," publicly calling for an end to the Vietnam War. They cut off their hair and donated it to the radical Black Panther Party. They also experimented with heroin and a radical form of psychotherapy. Many members of the press and public were dismayed by Lennon's varied and seemingly unfocused behavior. The *London Daily Mirror* called him "a not inconsiderable talent who seems to have gone completely off his rocker."[35]

Sessions for the next record, *Let It Be*, which was to be accompanied by a documentary film, were chaotic. The band members bickered with one another and fought over the direction of their joint business venture, Apple Corps. The album was put on hold and a new recording project began.

In the summer of 1969, they released *Abbey Road*, a miraculous model of cooperation and inspiration. Despite the record's generally sunny tone, however, Lennon was fed up. Weary of the pressure of being a Beatle and of the bickering that had replaced friendship,

After their marriage, Lennon and Yoko Ono held a "bed-in for peace," calling for an end to the Vietnam War.

Lennon announced that he wanted "a divorce." When the news became public, it stunned the world. The newspaper *New Musical Express* called it a sad end to "a musical fusion which wiped clean and drew again the face of pop music."[36]

Lennon's unhappiness had been clear for some time, so the announcement was not unexpected. Still, it was a sad day for once inseparable friends who had weathered hard times and sudden fame together.

The other Beatles felt they could not blame Lennon for pursuing what he wanted, because it had been his infectious energy and enthusiasm that had formed the band in the first place. McCartney later commented, "He wanted to live life, do stuff, and there was no holding back with John. And it was what we all admired him for. So we couldn't really say: 'Oh, we don't want you to do that, John. Stay with us.' You'd feel so wimpy."[37]

Imagine

Invigorated by his sudden freedom from the constraints of Beatle-hood, Lennon moved with his wife to New York City. He loved the city's vitality and creative ferment, which he compared to that of Liverpool.

At first Lennon was denied entry to America because of a 1968 British drug conviction. Even after he was allowed in, his petition to become a permanent resident was blocked by the government; alarmed by his radical leftist political connections, the government wanted to deport the singer. A four-year legal battle was required before Lennon was able to permanently settle in America.

During this time Lennon recorded as a solo artist, releasing such albums as the thoughtful *Imagine* and the heavily political *Some Time in New York City*. But the stress of the immigration battle caused Lennon to drink heavily and strained his marriage. The couple separated for about a year. The singer admitted later that Ono was right to make him leave: "I was behaving stupidly and I'd lost whatever it was about me that she found good in the first place. It was grow-up time and I'm glad she made me do it."[38]

Lennon spent most of this period of estrangement in Los Ange-les, soothing his loneliness by carousing with friends. Determined to make his marriage whole again, the singer eventually moved back

After separating from the Beatles, John Lennon moved to New York City with Yoko Ono.

to New York, gave up drugs except cigarettes and coffee, and reconciled with Ono. After moving back in, he ecstatically told reporters that the separation had been a failure.

With the birth of their son, Sean, late in 1975, Lennon more or less retired from public life. He stayed at home with the baby while Ono, an astute businesswoman, increased their wealth through investments. Although Lennon did not release a record for five years, he was never a total recluse; he traveled frequently and even renewed long-soured friendships with the other Beatles.

John Lennon was assassinated by Mark David Chapman on December 8, 1980.

When he did release another album, in 1980, it was a collaboration with Ono. *Double Fantasy* featured alternating tracks by husband and wife, and its message of domestic peace and fulfillment was a sharp contrast to the angrier, harsher songs, such as "Working Class Hero," that had been typical of his output earlier in his solo career.

A Hard World

The sense of peace conveyed by *Double Fantasy* was short-lived. On December 8, 1980, shortly after the singer's fortieth birthday, he was killed by a mentally disturbed fan. Mark David Chapman accosted Lennon as he returned home from a recording session, and shot him outside his apartment building. Lennon had given Chapman an autograph only hours earlier. The drifter, who later said he killed Lennon "to achieve fame" and "to be loved," is currently serving a life sentence for the crime.

The world was devastated by the loss. Yoko Ono's first public statement after the tragedy was simple and heartfelt: "John loved and prayed for the human race. Please do the same for him."[39]

Typical of the stunned reaction among fellow musicians was that of Bruce Springsteen. Springsteen was due to play a show in Philadelphia when the news struck. Members of his band were so upset they could barely take the stage, but the singer insisted. Speaking to the audience, Springsteen acknowledged his—and every rocker's—debt to the slain Lennon: "If it wasn't for John Lennon, a lot of us would be somewhere else tonight. It's a hard world that asks you to live with things that are unlivable, and it's hard to come out and play tonight, but there is nothing else to do."[40]

As a Beatle and as a solo artist, John Lennon brought rock to a new level of achievement. His collaborations with fellow Beatle Paul McCartney produced some of the most memorable and joyous pop songs ever written. His solo work, sometimes flawed but always impassioned, set a new standard for committed moral principles and intelligent lyrics in rock.

CHAPTER 4

Janis Joplin: Full-Tilt Boogie

"They're paying me $50,000 a year for me to be like me!"

—Janis Joplin

Janis Joplin was the premier white blues singer of the sixties, a larger-than-life performer of tremendous passion and nerve. Her music brought the rich emotions of the blues together with the mesmerizing energy of rock.

She rose to fame with Big Brother and the Holding Company, a band that symbolized the counterculture movement, during a time when the San Francisco Bay Area was the center of musical experimentation and the hippie life. Biographer Myra Friedman writes, "More than any performer of her day, she symbolized the mental condition of the decade that molded her genius, and out of its theatricalities, its eye-popping colors, its peaks [and low points] she made of herself a complete and dazzling original."[41]

In both positive and negative ways, Joplin was a role model for female musicians of future generations. When she began singing, there were almost no women in the all-boy club of top rock performers. Nonetheless, she rose from an unhappy, ugly-duckling childhood to become the club's queen. In so doing she proved that a woman, even one who

Janis Joplin overcame an unhappy childhood to become a rock legend.

was not conventionally beautiful, could join the club through talent and sheer force of will.

On- and offstage, Joplin also set the standard for a fundamental rock-and-roll icon: the tough-talking, hard-living blues mama. This brash image gradually took over the shy and sensitive aspects of Joplin's personality, and toward the end of her life, she showed her intelligent but fragile personal side less often. Many observers feel that Joplin's fast life and sometimes confused personality illustrate the best and worst about her generation: individual freedom and power, on the one hand, and self-indulgence and reckless experimentation, on the other.

Shaping an Image

Janis Lyn Joplin was born on January 19, 1943, the first child of Seth and Dorothy Joplin, in the dingy oil town of Port Arthur, Texas. Janis hated Port Arthur, a town that provided little cultural or intellectual stimulation. Furthermore, her home life was often difficult; the elder Joplins were distant with each other, with Janis, and with their other children. Things were no better at school, where weight and acne problems made Janis the brunt of teasing and insults. By the time she reached her teens, Janis had developed a fierce desire to leave.

Until she could make her getaway, Janis coped with her unhappiness by exaggerating her differences from the buttoned-down norm of 1950s Texas. Her manner was deliberately loud and abrasive. She refused to wear makeup, and she let her wavy hair grow unrestrained—shocking behavior in those days of heavy cosmetics and beehive hairdos.

The teenager was full of wild, unchanneled energy, and she demanded that her friends exist at the same intense level. Frank Davis, a sometime boyfriend, once remarked, "Janis could be adorable and incredibly lovable, but she would swat you like a cat playing with a mouse to get you angry, even violent, so you'd be at her level of passion."[42]

Janis's famous reputation for drinking, wild behavior and scandalously foul language began in her teens. Perhaps long before she consciously thought about becoming a music star, she began to form the outrageous behavior that later became a crucial part of her image. According to biographer Alice Echols, much of this wildness was not spontaneous but quite consciously created, as a way to rebel against the constraints of life in Port Arthur and the Joplin family: "The mythic Janis Joplin—the tough, raw, trashy broad—was a creature Janis began crafting as a teenager."[43]

Beginning to Sing

Janis spent a good deal of her high school years avoiding home; when she did go to the Joplin house, she always seemed to get into a fight with her parents. At one point, she became so difficult to deal with that the Joplins took the drastic step, shameful at that time and in that place, of sending their daughter to a psychologist.

Because Janis stayed away from home so much, she fell in with a group of friends who considered themselves Port Arthur's resident beatniks—intellectuals whose lives ran counter to the conformist tendencies of the 1950s. Janis was the only girl in this group.

As a teenager, Joplin wanted friends to feel the same passion she did.

She later recalled, "They read books and had ideas, and I started running around with them. We thought of ourselves as intellectuals, and I guess we were [considering the rest of] that place."[44]

Music played an important part in the lives of Port Arthur's beatniks, especially its only "beatnik chick." She listened avidly to old recordings of blues and folk singers. She took up the guitar and the autoharp to accompany herself as she tried to sing the songs she loved. Tentatively, Joplin began performing in public, taking the stage occasionally in Port Arthur's only coffee shop.

In particular, three singers influenced her deeply. One was bluesman Huddie Ledbetter, known as Leadbelly, a former convict who wrote such songs as "Goodnight, Irene" and "Rock Island Line." Another was folksinger Odetta, whose powerful voice popularized songs associated with the civil rights movement such as "Kumbaya." Most influential of all was blues singer Bessie Smith, about whom Janis once remarked: "She showed me the air and taught me how to fill it. She's the reason I started singing, really."[45]

Port Arthur to Austin to San Francisco

After graduating from high school, Joplin enrolled briefly in a local vocational college, but in the summer of 1961 she left Port Arthur for the University of Texas in Austin, a center for intellectuals and musicians. Janis fell in with Austin's other self-styled outcasts and let her inquisitive, rebellious side blossom. She experimented with drugs and sex, began drinking heavily, and developed a passion for literature, especially biographies and novels by writers like F. Scott Fitzgerald.

However, Joplin's university career lasted only a few months. She was too interested in Austin's music scene to take academics seriously. She sang whenever possible at open-mike nights in coffee shops and clubs, developing her voice into a powerful instrument that could hold the attention of an audience.

In 1963 a San Francisco concert promoter and native Texan, Chet Helms, heard Joplin in an Austin club and convinced her to come to San Francisco. He was impressed with her voice and thought she would have a great career in the San Francisco Bay Area. That region had long been a major center for beatnik life, but at the time it was evolving into something quite new: a center for what would eventually be called the Love Generation—the hippie generation.

Joplin adored San Francisco. The aspiring singer found sporadic work and collected unemployment; she was sometimes so poor that she was reduced to panhandling and shoplifting. Her life revolved around the Bay Area's folk and blues bars, and by word of mouth she gradually built up a reputation so strong that it sometimes scared the competition away. According to her friend Linda Gottfried, Joplin's voice was so powerful that "no other female singers wanted to sing when she showed up."[46]

Joining Big Brother

The man who had talked Joplin into coming to San Francisco, Chet Helms, was still convinced she could be a star. He decided to hook her up with friends who were in the rock band Big Brother and the Holding Company. Its psychedelic sound, focused on guitarist James Gurley's spacey solos, made the band a local favorite—but it needed a singer, and Helms thought Joplin fit the bill.

It was a new experience for Joplin. She had mostly performed as a solo act and had never sung in an electrified band. However, she later reflected, the singer felt as though she fit in from the first moments of her audition: "It happened the first time. I just exploded. I'd been into a Bessie Smith type thing. I stood still and I sang simple. But you can't sing like that in front of a rock band, all that rhythm and volume. You have to sing loud and move wild with all that in back of you."[47]

The band was impressed with the singer's forceful presence and hired her immediately. Guitarist Sam Andrew thought "she was really strong right away. Whether you liked her or not, you could tell that she was very extreme and unusual—a phenomenon."[48]

As word spread around town about Big Brother's dynamic new singer, Joplin replaced Gurley as the band's center attraction. Critics loved her; the enthusiasm of journalist Tom Wolfe was typical: "I had never heard such a voice or seen such a presentation. She was riveting."[49]

June 1967 was a major turning point for Joplin. It marked her now-famous performance at the Monterey Pop Festival, the first major outdoor rock festival. Her intense performance, preserved in the film *Monterey Pop*, stopped the show. Biographer Myra Friedman writes that Joplin's singing "shook with more energy than the rest of the entire festival. The roar that followed could have been a fissure opening in the earth."[50]

Breakup

Joplin became an instant legend at Monterey, and from then on she was in the international spotlight. Reporter after reporter interviewed her, usually while the singer sipped a bottle of Southern Comfort, her favorite drink. She was terrific "copy"—that is, she had all the elements of a great story. Nobody, especially a woman,

Janis Joplin with Big Brother and the Holding Company at the Monterey Pop Festival in 1967.

made as many outrageous, outspoken pronouncements as Janis Joplin. Many of her comments were X-rated; among the milder was "Onstage, I make love to 25,000 people—then I go home alone."[51]

Columbia Records immediately offered the band a contract. *Cheap Thrills*, released in July 1968, sold a million copies in a month and stayed in the number one slot for eight weeks. *Cheap Thrills* has many high points, including a fierce interpretation of the blues classic "Ball and Chain." Many felt the album was only partly successful, however, because it failed to capture the emotional power of the singer's live performance.

Even before the album's release, the focus on Joplin and her overnight success at Monterey was creating tension between her and the band. The lavish attention on the singer also brought the rest of Big Brother under scrutiny, and the other musicians were savagely attacked as unequal to her talent. At first reluctant to heed the many calls for her to quit the band, Joplin eventually decided that it was

The praise Joplin received for her performance at the Monterey Pop Festival led to her eventual split from Big Brother.

more important to find adequate backup than to remain loyal to her friends.

She left Big Brother less than a month after the release of *Cheap Thrills*. The split was a wrenching experience for Joplin. "It was a very sad thing, man," the singer told a reporter. "I love those guys more than anybody else in the whole world, they know that. But if I had any serious idea of myself as a musician, I had to leave."[52]

From Kozmic to Full Tilt

Now officially a solo artist, Joplin decided that her next band would emulate the horn-rich bands of classic soul singers like Aretha Franklin and Wilson Pickett. (Soul was an influential style of black popular music that had evolved out of the rhythm and blues of the 1950s.)

Her new band, the Kozmic Blues Band, was made up of seasoned studio musicians, with Sam Andrew the only holdover from Big Brother. The group never took off, however. Its debut, at the annual convention of a Memphis soul music label in December 1968, was a disaster. The hastily assembled group could not compete with such polished groups as the Staple Singers or Booker T. and the MGs. In San Francisco, in front of a crowd of adoring hippies, Joplin might have gotten away with a sloppy performance, but not in Memphis, a hotbed of ultra-tight, sophisticated soul. The audience was unresponsive, and the singer bombed. Joplin wryly commented, "At least they didn't throw things."[53]

Matters did not improve over time. The band was too big, with busy arrangements that deflected the focus from Joplin. Furthermore, high turnover and personal tensions prevented it from becoming a cohesive unit. Making the band's only record, 1969's *I Got Dem Ol' Kozmic Blues Again Mama!*, was an unpleasant experience. Bassist Brad Campbell recalled, "Everybody was putting down everybody else. It was a mess, a total mess."[54]

By early 1970 Joplin replaced the Kozmic Blues Band with another group, the Full Tilt Boogie Band. Full Tilt was sparer in its instrumentation, its richness coming from a piano-and-organ combination similar to those in many gospel groups. In the opinion of many critics and fans, it was the most competent and responsive of all of Joplin's backups.

Pearl

Joplin had long presented two separate faces to the world. One was the public Janis: the hard-drinking, red-hot mama that journalists loved to write about. This persona was nicknamed Pearl.

While the public saw Janis Joplin as a hard-drinking party-lover, her friends knew that the "real" Janis was fragile and insecure.

The other was the "real" Janis, intelligent but with a fragile, insecure side. This was the side that friends saw. Linda Gravenites, a close friend who made many of Joplin's flamboyant stage costumes, recalled being with Joplin when the singer was reading an article about herself: "Suddenly, she looked up and said, 'My God, what if they find out I'm only Janis!'"[55]

The two halves of Joplin's personality sometimes changed places with startling speed. Journalist David Henderson notes, "She could sound like a university-educated Texas schoolteacher one minute, and an insane, lascivious teenager the next."[56]

As her fame increased, the real Janis became increasingly rare. Since the world expected her to be sassy Pearl, few people saw anything else. As Pearl, Joplin pursued action as hard as possible. This meant, among other things, nonstop rounds of serious partying, drinking, and drug use. The singer often talked about how a few years of "superhypermost" living was preferable to a long but uneventful life.

Oddly for someone who was an icon of the LSD era, Joplin never cared for the mind-expanding qualities of psychedelic drugs. She said she wanted to obliterate her reality, not heighten it. Nothing helped her avoid reality better than heroin, and by 1970 Joplin was a full-blown addict.

Joplin's friends worried about her increasingly self-destructive lifestyle and her apparent inability to separate her public persona from her private life. When they suggested that she act more like herself in public, she replied: "That stuff made me famous! Everybody loves it."[57]

"Drinks Are On Pearl"

The pursuit of "superhypermost" living finally proved to be too much. On October 4, 1970, Joplin's body was found in her room at the Landmark Hotel in Hollywood, where she had been staying while recording a new album, *Pearl*. She was facedown on the floor, with fresh puncture marks in her arm. She was twenty-seven. Despite widespread speculation that she had committed suicide, and even that she had been murdered, Joplin's death was ruled an accidental drug overdose.

The singer died just before recording a vocal for the song "Buried Alive in the Blues." The backing track, which had already been taped, appears as an instrumental on the posthumously released *Pearl*. The absence of her voice is a mute memorial to her.

Death often makes celebrities even bigger than they had been before death, and the album was a huge success financially. It spent nine weeks at the number one spot. Its high point is the bittersweet song "Me and Bobby McGee," which ironically became Joplin's first chart-topping single as a solo artist—after her death.

As her fame grew, Joplin's drinking, partying, and drug use increased in frequency.

According to her wishes, Joplin was cremated and her ashes scattered from a plane along the coast of Marin County, near San Francisco. Joplin's will authorized money for a wake to be held in her honor. Invitations to the party, which was attended by dozens of friends and associates, read: "Drinks are on Pearl."

The Joplin legacy lives on, because she was one of the biggest female stars of her time and an icon of the volatile '60s: half hard-shelled blues mama, half vulnerable flower child. Her insistence on working as an equal within the male-dominated music scene also made her a role model for generations of female singers who followed.

CHAPTER 5

Jimi Hendrix: Guitar Warrior-Poet

> "Hendrix created a branch on the pop tree that nobody else has ventured too far out on. None has actually extended the directions he pursued, but perhaps that is because he took them, in his painfully short time on earth, as far as they could go."
>
> —critic John Morthland

Jimi Hendrix was perhaps the most innovative and influential guitarist who ever lived. He expanded the potential of his instrument in new and astonishing ways, redefining guitar technique and setting bold new standards. His commitment to experimentation constantly pushed the envelope of what rock could and should be about.

Many consider Jimi Hendrix one of the most influential guitarists who ever lived.

The Hendrix legend also rests on a flamboyant take-no-prisoners stage presence. He played his guitars with his teeth and behind his back, he caressed them like lovers, and sometimes he violently smashed and burned them.

His larger-than-life stage persona and his offstage personal manner were often at odds. He was famous for playing aggressively, but he also wrote beautiful slow ballads. Although he was famous for crudely screeching feedback and torched guitars, he also made significant contributions to sophisticated studio techniques. He took the stage like a wild man, but in private was intensely spiritual, soft-spoken, and shy.

This spiritual aspect of music was extremely important to Hendrix. He preferred not talking about his music, letting it speak for itself, but sometimes he tried to articulate his feelings. He remarked in a 1969 interview, "A musician, if he's a messenger, is like a child who hasn't been handled too many times by man, hasn't had too many fingerprints across his brain. That's why music is so much heavier than anything [else] you ever felt."[58]

Learning the Blues

Hendrix was born in Seattle, Washington, on November 27, 1942. He was of mixed white, black, and Cherokee blood. Journalist Charles Shaar Murray comments that this mixture made the guitarist "a real American, with the history of his nation imprinted in his genes."[59]

After their parents separated, Jimmy (as his name was spelled then) and his younger brother, Leon, were raised by their hardworking, serious-minded father, Al.

Jimmy was a shy, introverted child who spent a lot of time reading. Science fiction was an early passion, and references to other worlds would often appear in his songwriting later. Biographers Harry Shapiro and Caesar Glebbeek write, "The nature of the universe would take on great significance for him within his own personal cosmology."[60]

Another passion was music. After Jimmy got in trouble with his father for wrecking a broom while pretending it was a guitar, he begged his father for a real guitar. Al found him a cast-off ukelele and, later, a series of cheap guitars.

Though left-handed, Jimmy never used guitars designed for left-handers. He restrung right-hand models and played them upside down. Nor did he ever have formal lessons. His father recalled, "We didn't have that kind of money. So he just taught himself. He just picked it up. It was just in him, and the guitar became another part of his anatomy."[61]

Jimmy first learned guitar by playing along with his father's collection of blues records by musicians like Muddy Waters and B. B. King. He once remarked, "The first guitarist I was aware of was Muddy Waters. I heard one of his old records when I was a little boy and it scared me to death."[62]

In high school Jimmy became involved in Seattle's teen dance scene. He played in several bands and jammed with anyone who

Jimmy received his first guitar lessons by listening to albums recorded by B. B. King and Muddy Waters (pictured).

would let him onstage. He sometimes took only a hamburger as payment. And he practiced incessantly; all the Hendrix neighbors knew the strange, shy kid who walked around the neighborhood fingering the guitar around his neck.

Absorbing Influences

Hendrix dropped out of high school and enlisted in the army in 1959 or 1960 (accounts vary). Many of his fellow paratroopers in the 101st Airborne found him strange. He slept with his guitar and talked about using it to capture the sounds he heard in his head, such as air rushing past his ears when he parachuted.

He was stationed near Nashville, and after his discharge in 1962 settled there to lead a dance band, the King Kasuals, under the name Jimmy James. "You really had to play, 'cos those people were really hard to please," the guitarist later recalled of audiences in Nashville, the capital of country music. "That's where I learned to play really."[63]

In addition to appearing in front of tough Nashville audiences with his own band, Hendrix also worked on the road in other groups. He toured the South with such classic R&B, soul, and blues artists as Sam Cooke, B. B. King, Little Richard, Jackie Wilson, the Isley Brothers, Ike and Tina Turner, and Wilson Pickett. This experience gave Hendrix a working knowledge of black musical styles far beyond what records could teach him. It also gave him something else: invaluable performance skills. By watching what the stars of the shows did to entertain an audience, Hendrix began to form his own ideas of showmanship.

On tour with other musicians, Hendrix learned black music styles and what it took to entertain an audience.

According to biographer David Henderson, Hendrix's wild stage presence began to develop during this period. "He did flip-flops, played the guitar behind his back, ate the strings, and did splits—all at the same time, it seemed. He had a ribbon tied to his arm and one tied to his leg, and he wore an earring in one ear and had an outrageous pompadour."[64]

New York

Deciding the time was right to go for the big time, Hendrix moved to New York City's Greenwich Village around 1964. The Village was then a hotbed of musical ferment, with dozens of performers experimenting in a variety of blues, folk, and rock idioms. They provided a new set of influences for Hendrix; he was especially influenced by the lyric writing of Bob Dylan, then the king of folk music, and began incorporating Dylan-style poetic imagery in his own songs. Take, for example, the impressionistic style of his song "May This Be Love," which uses images of waterfalls and rainbows to invoke a mystical love for a woman.

Hendrix formed an innovative blues band, Jimmy James and the Blue Flames. He used it as a vehicle for his own compositions and experiments with new forms of electronics like wa-wa pedals, which distort the usual sound of guitars. Onstage he produced eerie sounds no one had ever heard before, startling audiences with sonic effects like feedback. He also put on a wild performance, with onstage antics he'd learned on the road. He played the guitar with his teeth or behind his back; he gently caressed his guitar or hurled it violently around; he stormed ferociously around the stage.

As word spread about Hendrix, celebrities dropped by clubs to check him out. Among them were jazz trumpeter Miles Davis, members of the Rolling Stones, and Mike Bloomfield, then the star of the well-known Paul Butterfield Blues Band. Bloomfield recalled his first exposure to the virtuoso guitarist: "I was the hottest guitarist on the block—I thought I was *it*. Hendrix knew who I was, and that day, in front of my eyes, he burned me to death. I didn't even get my guitar out. H-bombs were going off, guided missiles were flying. . . . I didn't even want to pick up a guitar for the next year."[65]

London

Another musician who noticed Hendrix was Chas Chandler, formerly the bassist for a British Invasion group, the Animals. Chandler offered to manage Hendrix. Assuring Hendrix that he would be a star in England, he convinced the guitarist to move to London in 1966.

The timing was perfect. The Beatles had stopped touring, and the London scene was eager to embrace new talent. The British pop audience's obsession with blues and R&B, which had begun with bands like the Rolling Stones, was peaking. The time was right for someone who could blend the emotion of the blues and the showmanship of R&B with the polish of pop, the eloquence of folk, and the power of rock.

At the suggestion of Chandler and his partner, Michael Jeffrey, Hendrix used his real surname again and began spelling his first name more exotically. When they hooked the guitarist up with two Englishmen, bassist Noel Redding and drummer Mitch Mitchell, the Jimi Hendrix Experience was born.

The band focused on ultra-loud performance and a wild appearance, with frizzed-out hair and outlandish clothes. The main draw, however, was always Hendrix. Audiences were mesmerized by his presence, which was both spiritual and sensual, and his extraordinary guitar work, which combined his virtuoso technique with a deep knowledge of the blues and a deafening rock sound.

The guitarist burst on the London pop scene like a bombshell and was its undisputed king just six months after his arrival. He became the

Despite the loud performances and outrageous look of the Jimi Hendrix Experience, Hendrix himself was the main attraction.

rage of pop society, praised by celebrities like Paul McCartney, guitarist Eric Clapton of Cream, and Rolling Stone member Brian Jones. His first singles, "Hey Joe" and "Purple Haze," and a subsequent album, *Are You Experienced?*, were huge hits.

Back to America

American audiences had not yet heard the Experience except through records, and his first performance back in his native land was eagerly anticipated. It occurred at the same festival where Janis Joplin became a star: the Monterey Pop Festival.

This performance (preserved, like Joplin's, in the film *Monterey Pop*) became

After returning from England, Hendrix's first performance was at the Monterey Pop Festival.

instantly famous. The guitarist was at his wildest, capping the ferocious set by burning his instrument onstage. Hendrix was unlike anything anyone had ever seen, and he more than fulfilled the stories that had preceded him. The *Los Angeles Times* noted in its review of the festival that by the time Hendrix left the stage, he "had graduated from rumor to legend."[66]

Following Monterey, Hendrix moved back to New York and continued to record and tour to ecstatic crowds. But as his fame grew, he became increasingly unhappy. He considered himself a musician first and a star second, and he felt trapped by his stereotyped public persona—the wild man who played screaming rock, dressed outrageously, and performed flamboyantly. He decided to drop the flashy trappings and simply play his music.

Audiences met these stripped-down shows with hostility, and Hendrix was surprised and disappointed. He began to withdraw from live performance and concentrated instead on a new state-of-the-art studio, Electric Ladyland, that he built in Manhattan.

He spent hundreds of hours there, playing with friends like jazz guitarist John McLaughlin. Hendrix also loved to visit clubs, letting his ideas flow freely by jamming (improvising) with different players.

He once remarked, "Any chance we have, we jam. That's what playing's all about . . . when you're creating music with other musicians. That's what you live for."[67]

New Directions

The guitarist's new, less commercial direction met with resistance. His management was especially unhappy, since Hendrix's move away from a tried-and-true formula meant fewer record and ticket sales.

Meanwhile, a militant African American group, the Black Panthers, was also applying pressure. The Panthers wanted Hendrix to play "blacker" music that was overtly political in nature, using his celebrity for their cause. The guitarist resisted this, however, saying that he was uninterested in politics and color-blind in his personal relations.

By the summer of 1969, his band collapsed under the pressures. Hendrix retreated to upstate New York and gathered around him a loose affiliation of players ranging from bluesmen to avant-garde classical composers. He called them his "electric family" or "electric sky church."

Part of this "electric family" appeared when Hendrix closed the Woodstock festival that summer with a stunning version of "The Star-Spangled Banner"—a performance many consider the high point of his career. Captured in the film *Woodstock*, it has done much to further his legend in the years since. Biographer Charles Shaar Murray notes, "It was both a performance which no other living musician would have been capable of conceiving or executing, and a graphic demonstration that Hendrix's artistic ambitions had grown in proportion to—but in a radically different direction from—his immense popularity."[68]

The End

Hendrix was searching for a new direction but seemed unable to find one. Late in 1969 he debuted a new trio, Band of Gypsys, with bassist Billy Cox and drummer Buddy Miles. The band was short-lived, however. Early in 1970 Hendrix walked offstage midway through a show, allegedly because some bad LSD made him sick, and the trio never played again. When the guitarist performed again in public, it was with Cox and Experience drummer Mitchell.

Hendrix's musical explorations sometimes took him afar. For instance, he traveled to Hawaii to take part in a project called the Rainbow Bridge Vibratory Color/Sound Experiment. This event, a chaotic project organized by a mystical religious group, included a concert held at the base of a volcano. However, Hendrix spent most of his time at home or in the studio, trying to reproduce the sounds

Jimi Hendrix closed the Woodstock festival with a stunning rendition of "The Star-Spangled Banner."

he heard in his head.

On the morning of September 18, 1970, in the wake of a chaotic European tour with Mitchell and Cox, Hendrix took nine sleeping pills and went to bed at the London home of girlfriend Monika Danneman. Late that day Danneman found him unconscious. Danneman summoned an ambulance, but Hendrix was dead on arrival at the hospital. He was twenty-seven years old.

The official declaration concerning his death was an open verdict. That is, the London coroner ruled out murder but could not rule conclusively that his death was either suicide or an accident. Many observers have speculated in the years since about the case. As a result, critic John Morthland writes, "his death has only deepened the mystery and confusion, only reinforced his image as a freak genius."[69]

Tributes and Legacies

The millions of fans devoted to the innovative, charismatic guitarist were stunned by his death. Tributes from musical colleagues,

In the midst of a European tour, Jimi Hendrix passed away at his girlfriend's London home on September 18, 1970.

fans, and critics were heartfelt. Michael Lydon summed up critical feelings when he wrote in the *New York Times*, "He was an artist extravagantly generous with his beauty."[70]

Hendrix's friends and fellow musicians were equally saddened. Many years later his friend guitarist Carlos Santana remarked that his premature death "was a combination of the lifestyle—staying up all night, chicks, too much drugs, all kinds of stuff. It was a combination of all the intensities he felt, along with a lack of discipline. In the rock style of life at that time, there was no discipline."[71]

The Hendrix family abandoned tentative plans for an all-star memorial in Seattle in favor of a quiet funeral. The service was simple; a longtime family friend sang gospel hymns and family members read poems and eulogies. Hendrix was buried in Greenwood Cemetery in Renton, a suburb of Seattle, on September 29. It was just shy of the guitarist's twenty-eighth birthday.

In the years since, his legacy and legend have been kept alive in many ways. Hundreds of hours of recorded material, unreleased in his lifetime, have been best-sellers. Films of him in performance are perennial hits. His shows have inspired at least one full-time impersonator. Hendrix serves as the core spirit and inspiration for Experience Music Project, an innovative music museum in Seattle. And guitarists throughout the world continue to acknowledge the influence of the innovative guitarist who was both a musical warrior and a mystical poet.

CHAPTER 6

Bruce Springsteen: The Boss

"Once I found the guitar, I had the key to the highway."

—Bruce Springsteen

Bruce Springsteen was a cult favorite—a legend to a select few—for years before he broke into the stratosphere of massive popularity and superstardom. Springsteen's powerful albums and energetic live shows were unpretentious alternatives to the bland, commercial face of rock of the 1970s and 1980s. When he burst on the national consciousness in the mid-1970s, America was exhausted by the long battles of Vietnam and Watergate; President Jimmy Carter spoke publicly of "an age of malaise." Pop music, reflecting this feeling, had been offering mainly shallow escapism. It was an opportune time for Springsteen's refreshingly honest voice and emotionally generous live shows.

In addition to being considered by many one of the most consistently strong and passionate performers in rock, Springsteen is known as a gifted and prolific songwriter. Although some of his earlier songs can be wordy and overly complicated, his mature songs show him to be a plainspoken rock visionary. They comprise an epic, sweeping vision of America. Individually, they explore the hopes and dreams of everyday lives, especially those of the

Bruce Springsteen is considered one of the most passionate rock performers.

country's small-town, working-class heartland. Springsteen's songs speak to millions because they describe the heroic in the lives and dreams of ordinary people. His steady commitment to causes advocating social justice has also endeared him to millions of fans.

Springsteen has always carried the torch for one of rock's most basic elements: a passionate belief in the music as a source of personal redemption. Springsteen has often stated that rock and roll saved him from a life of bitterness and despair, and his belief that it can save others has never wavered.

Perhaps the keys to understanding Springsteen's appeal and personality are his powerfully charismatic belief in himself and in rock, a serious-minded faith in hard work and perseverence, and a regular-guy jauntiness. He once raved to an audience, "I have been reborn, rededicated, resuscitated, reinvigorated, and rejuvenated with the magic, the mystery, and the ministry of rock and roll. . . . I don't know what to say except that I'm real happy."[72]

Freehold

Springsteen's songs often concern the dreams of hardworking, blue-collar men and women, and he comes by this material honestly. He was born in the factory town of Freehold, New Jersey, on September 23, 1949, as the first child of Douglas and Adele Springsteen. Freehold's gritty atmosphere, and the hopes and despairs of his father's working life, would one day profoundly affect Springsteen's music.

Douglas Springsteen held a variety of jobs, including prison guard and bus driver. His frequent periods of unemployment left him bitter and disillusioned, according to his son; in contrast, Adele Springsteen, a legal secretary, was a constant source of vitality and optimism. "My mother is the great energy—she's the energy of the show," the singer once remarked. "The consistency, the steadiness, day after day—that's her. And the refusal to be disheartened."[73]

Douglas wanted his boy to go to college and become a lawyer, but Bruce had other ideas. After hearing rockers like Elvis, he was too attached to rock and roll. Music promised an escape from Freehold and a dreary life of factory work. "The first day I can remember looking in a mirror and being able to stand what I was seeing," the singer recalled, "was the day I had a guitar in my hand."[74]

His mother bought him his first electric guitar for $18, amplifier included. Bruce spent all of his free time practicing, and friends recall he was not interested in sports, dating, or other aspects of teenage life. A fast learner, within a year Springsteen was playing lead guitar for a teen dance band called the Castiles. The band played anywhere it could: high school dances, supermarket open-

Bruce Springsteen (far right) first played lead guitar for the Castiles.

ings, and, Springsteen recalled, even an asylum for the mentally disturbed: "This guy in a suit got up and introduced us for twenty minutes, saying we were greater than the Beatles. Then the doctors came up and took him away."[75]

The Nucleus of Stardom

Bruce's commitment to music led to bitter conflicts with his father. They fought about the loudness of Bruce's guitar, about Bruce's hair length, about Bruce's direction in life. In concert, the singer later introduced songs about father-son conflicts by remarking, "When I was growing up, there were two things that were unpopular in my house: One was me, the other was my guitar."[76]

After high school graduation in 1967, Springsteen briefly attended community college. When his family moved to California, he stayed in Asbury Park, a seedy but colorful beach resort near Freehold, and played in a succession of bar bands. (At some point during this period, the guitarist was nicknamed "the Boss," a title he has never liked.) Springsteen was still developing his singing at this point, but his fluent lead guitar work always made him the center of attention. "Put him onstage with a guitar," a friend recalled, "and he lit it up. It was like somebody had plugged him in."[77]

The most significant of these bands was Steel Mill, which featured Bruce as guitarist, singer, and, increasingly, composer. After it disbanded in 1971, he formed the Bruce Springsteen Band, which included Steel Mill alumni Vini Lopez on drums and Danny Federici on organ. It was rounded out by pianist David Sancious, bassist Garry Tallent, and a pro footballer turned tenor saxophonist, Clarence "Big Man" Clemons. This was the basis of the band that would back Springsteen as he became a star.

When Springsteen signed a contract with Columbia Records, Columbia decided to ignore his roots in rock. Instead, it emphasized his songwriting, which relied heavily on colorful characters drawn from his Jersey Coast days. He was promoted as a "new Dylan"— a sensitive singer/songwriter, not a rocker—for his first albums, *Greetings from Asbury Park, NJ* and *The Wild, the Innocent and the E Street Shuffle*.

The Perfect Backup

The singer toured nonstop and built a loyal following, mainly on the East Coast, who raved about his three- or four-hour shows. Word slowly built about him until things took a dramatic turn in April 1974. An influential critic, Jon Landau, caught a show in Cambridge, Massachusetts. Landau raved in print that "I saw rock and roll's future, and its name is Bruce Springsteen."[78] Columbia Records used the quote in a major ad campaign and album sales jumped.

He appeared to be on the brink of major success, but Springsteen hit a snag while completing his third album. He was obsessed with fine-tuning every detail and with forming a unifying sweep of ideas to link each song. "The album became a monster," he recalled. "It wanted everything. It just ate up everyone's life."[79]

Landau had been visiting the New York studio where the singer was working, offering suggestions and encouragement, and Springsteen asked him to coproduce the stalled record. Landau's input proved vital to completing it, and Landau remained a crucial part of Springsteen's creative team for years.

Several personnel changes added further strength to the mix: "Miami" Steve Van Zandt, Springsteen's oldest friend from the Asbury Park days, joined as rhythm guitarist. Drummer Max E. Weinberg replaced Lopez, and pianist Roy Bittan replaced Sancious. This completed the "classic" lineup of the E Street Band. Springsteen would no doubt have become a star even without them; nonetheless, he now had the perfect backup. Van Zandt and Clemons, for example, served as Springsteen's onstage theatrical partners during the elaborate, funny stories he used to introduce each song.

More Than Just a Good Time

During the long months Springsteen was in the studio, anticipation about the singer built to a fever pitch, especially after *Time* and *Newsweek* ran simultaneous cover stories on him focusing on the making of the new star. Within a month of its release in October 1975, *Born to Run*, which many consider Springsteen's finest album, reached number three on the charts. The title song became Springsteen's first hit single.

During his first national tour, audiences responded rapturously to the singer's intense charisma and theatricality. Sandwiched between his impassioned songs, Springsteen's long, often invented stories became nearly as entertaining as his music. The singer made sure that everyone behind him, from the band to the lighting crew, stayed razor-sharp and followed him perfectly. And the music, a mix of originals and rock classics, moved easily from intimacy to joyous, explosive rock. It seemed to many that Springsteen had tapped into the pure spirit of rock and roll.

His shows had always been generous in length. They often lasted three or four hours, with encore after encore. Springsteen felt an obligation, he said, to give fans their money's worth: "I want to be able to go home and say I went all the way tonight—and then I went a little further."[80]

Pictured with Bruce Springsteen is his long-time backup, the E Street Band.

His goal, however, was to deliver more than just a good time. Springsteen's stories and songs were couched in good-time, blue-collar images of cars and girls. But they also dealt with ambitious themes like love, brotherhood, honor and duty, hope and despair. Rock was fun, Springsteen was saying, but it was also capable of conveying serious ideas.

Recordings

Just as Springsteen's success was skyrocketing, the juggernaut slowed. He discovered that his manager, Mike Appel, had been exploiting him financially. In the spring of 1976 Springsteen sued Appel, alleging fraud and breach of trust. Appel retaliated by legally barring Landau from producing Springsteen. Since Springsteen wanted to record only with Landau, the standoff kept the singer out of the studio for a year.

The somber mood of *Darkness on the Edge of Town*, Springsteen's first album after the layoff, reflects this troubled period. Its stories of shattered dreams powerfully convey a mixture of faith and resignation. Critic Hugh Wilson notes, "There was hope in the record, and some of the desire of youth remained, but it was a fragile hope that had to be fought for."[81]

The singer's next releases were a double album, *The River*, which gave Springsteen's serious lyrics an overlay of bright, radio-friendly pop music sound, and then a starkly acoustic album, *Nebraska*, which was recorded almost entirely solo at Springsteen's New Jersey home. They sold only moderately well, especially the deliberately noncommercial *Nebraska*, and some observers speculated that Springsteen had run his course.

But then, in 1984 Springsteen decided to go in the opposite direction. He crafted an album, *Born in the U.S.A.*, that he hoped would intentionally capture a mass audience. "There was a value in trying to connect with a large audience," he explained later. "It was a direct way you could affect culture. It let you know how powerful and durable your music might be."[82]

Born in the U.S.A.

His plan worked. Tickets became so hard to get for Springsteen shows that law firms used them as enticements for young recruits. *Born in the U.S.A.* was a commercial smash. It stayed in the top ten for two years and produced a seemingly endless string of hit singles. *Born in the U.S.A.* cemented Springsteen's place in rock's major leagues and his role as a major creative voice.

The reason for the album's success was its combination of catchiness and content. Each song had a catchy melody and an irresistible "hook"—a musical figure or chorus that catches the ear and stays in the memory. Often they seemed nothing more than light-weight pop tunes; but there was more beneath the surface. Fans who listened to Springsteen's pared-down lyrics heard his continuing preoccupation with the dark side of the American dream.

For example, on first listen the title song seems to be a light tune with a great hook and a patriotic, catchy chorus repeating "born in the U.S.A." Closer listening, however, reveals it to be deeply ironic. It is a story narrated by a disillusioned, bitter Vietnam veteran who feels betrayed after risking his life for his country and

Springsteen performs his hit song "Born in the U.S.A."

seeing many of his friends killed. He returns home to find little more than loneliness, frustration, and lost opportunity.

The combination of catchy pop and serious content was gold, and it gave birth to a phenomenon the media dubbed Bossmania. Bossmania combined a frenzy of patriotic feeling (fueled by the album's title song) with fever over Springsteen himself, who had traded in his scrawny Jersey-rat looks for a new, buffed-up physique. Journalist Parke Puterbaugh comments, *"Born in the U.S.A.* wasn't just an album and tour but a seismic event in the rock & roll timeline."[83]

Social Concerns

The album's serious subject matter was so well hidden beneath its bright surface that Springsteen's messages were often misinterpreted. During the 1984 presidential campaign, for example, incumbent Ronald Reagan wrongly cited the song as being patriotic, then referred to "the message of hope in songs of a man so many young Americans admire: New Jersey's own Bruce Springsteen."[84]

Springsteen, a lifelong Democrat, did not comment directly on the Republican president's misinterpretation of his message. However, in the wake of *Born in the U.S.A.*, the singer did increase his speaking out on social and political concerns. He had long wanted his music to "be useful," a positive element in the minds and lives of listeners. Journalist Eric Alterman asserts that Springsteen "is just about the most socially empathetic star the business has ever produced."[85]

Springsteen used his fame as a means to further his causes. He performed dozens of benefits for Vietnam veterans' groups. He do-

Springsteen performs alongside E Street Band member Clarence Clemons during the Born in the U.S.A. *tour.*

nated to social service and environmental agencies in each city he played. He performed on the charity single "We Are the World" and headlined Amnesty International's Human Rights Now! tours.

He also spoke out onstage, urging his fans to think, learn, and act for themselves. "The world is nothing but complex," Springsteen remarked, "and if you do not learn to interpret its complexities, you're going to be on the river without a paddle."[86]

Personal Concerns

Springsteen had always been too focused on his career to sustain a long-term relationship. That changed during the height of Bossmania, when he met and married model and actress Julianne Phillips. The singer joked that he was merely obeying the wishes of his Italian grandmother, who wanted him to settle down. The ceremony was held in Phillips's home town of Lake Oswego, Oregon, causing one journalist to crack that it was Oregon's biggest news story since Lewis and Clark.

Springsteen's next recording (not counting a concert compilation) reflected his new status as husband. *Tunnel of Love*, released in 1987 as the performer approached forty, was his most personal and intimate statement to date. Many of its comments about the difficulties of keeping love alive proved poignantly true: the singer's marriage, a victim of conflicting careers and temperaments, was falling apart.

Meanwhile, a new love was on the horizon. The centerpieces of Springsteen's shows had become the tender onstage interactions between him and backup singer Patti Scialfa. Scialfa, who had joined the band for the *Born in the U.S.A.* tour, was, like Springsteen, a Jersey native of Irish Italian extraction. "They weren't just acting" onstage, according to biographer Dave Marsh. "They'd fallen in love in real life."[87]

Phillips filed for divorce, and Springsteen married Scialfa in 1991. The couple now has three children and homes in Los Angeles and New Jersey. The singer seems to have succeeded in balancing stardom with sanity and rock life with normal life. He understands now, he says, that family is as important as music: "Two of the best days in my life were the day I picked up the guitar and the day I learned how to put it down."[88]

Musically, Springsteen has also changed in the years since *Born in the U.S.A.* made him a superstar. The biggest change involved dissolving his longtime backup, the E Street Band, in 1989. He commented that it was time for a change: "You can get to a place where you start to replay the ritual, and nostalgia creeps in."[89]

After divorcing Julianne Phillips, Springsteen married backup singer Patti Scialfa (pictured) in 1991.

Springsteen's subsequent albums and tours have received mixed reviews. However, in 1999 the event Springsteen fans had been waiting for—a reunion tour with the E Street Band—sold out in record-breaking time and received strong reviews. The following year, his song "American Skin (41 Shots)," about a controversial police killing, drew protests from police organizations across the country and proved that he is still capable of writing hard-hitting songs with thoughtful content. The singer may have semiretired into family life, but the Springsteen legend is still alive and growing.

CHAPTER 7

Johnny Rotten:
King of Punk

"You should never, ever be understood completely. That's like the kiss of death, isn't it?"

—Johnny Rotten

John Lydon, better known as Johnny Rotten, contributed little to rock and roll in traditional terms. He performed in relatively few live shows and made only a handful of records. But as the vocalist, lyricist, and frontman for the Sex Pistols, Rotten symbolized a movement that profoundly affected rock. Provocative, angry, and deliberately mysterious, he was the most visible symbol of the punk revolution of 1976–77—the emblem of a short-lived but influential musical style that turned rock on its head.

By writing and singing about a world that offered "No Future" (the title of one of his songs), Rotten crystallized the diminished dreams of young working-class people in England. His angry lyrics and sly, outrageous personality epitomized their rage against Britain's social injustices and unfair class system. Rotten also became a hero to the American branch of the punk movement. He has continued to be a provocative and outspoken critic of music and society in the years since the Pistols exploded on the scene and just as quickly self-destructed.

Musically, Rotten's band was important because it stripped rock back to its crudest fundamentals, forcing a return to its roots. Punk featured flailing guitars, rough rhythms, and screaming vocals. It was raw, abrasive, and basic, just as rock and roll had been in its beginnings. This roughness was a deliberate spit in the collective eye of those producing the commercial, bland, overly produced mainstream rock of the 1970s.

Moreover, by challenging established practices of making music, Rotten spearheaded a new attitude toward its production. Punk was all about democracy. Anyone could get up onstage; it hardly mattered if you could play. By extension, anyone could produce and distribute

Johnny Rotten's brand of punk rock was similar to early rock and roll: raw, abrasive, and basic.

a record or promote a concert. This independent, do-it-yourself style of music production, often avoiding the mainstream music industry entirely, was a revolutionary idea that has become standard operating procedure for many musicians in the years since.

Street Kid

John Joseph Lydon's rough upbringing began when he was born in London, England, probably on January 31, 1956. In his autobiography, he states that the date is uncertain because his birth certificate was accidentally destroyed and no one in his family remembers the precise date.

The Lydons lived in North Finsbury, a tough neighborhood. Johnny's father, John Christopher Lydon, was a crane operator; his mother, Eileen, was ill through most of John's childhood. Johnny was the family cook and the nursemaid for his three younger brothers.

At age seven Johnny developed spinal meningitis and was hospitalized for a year, six months of which was spent in and out of a coma. The disease left him with a hunched back and, according to his autobiography, memory loss that required the relearning of basic school knowledge.

Chronic health problems have continued to plague him into adulthood, including severe headaches, occasional epileptic seizures, and poor eyesight. Rotten says the "Rotten stare," his famously unblinking gaze, is not a deliberate attempt to unnerve people but simply an attempt to see clearly.

Johnny was always an indifferent and defiant student, and he was expelled from school at fifteen for bad behavior. He moved out of his parents' house into an illegal squat (condemned building). His chief passions were football (which Americans call soccer) and music, especially hard-edged, metallic rockers like Alice Cooper, Hawkwind, and T. Rex.

He held brief jobs, including working at a day-care center and cleaning the houses of the wealthy. But Lydon's primary activity was busking, or street performing, in subway stations. With his friend John Ritchie, later known as Sid Vicious, flailing away on guitar, Lydon would saw away at a violin and scream lyrics from the only song he knew: Alice Cooper's "I Love the Dead." The duo's sound was so unique that people paid them to move away. Lydon noted wryly: "Sid couldn't play guitar and I couldn't play violin, but we had the most fun."[90]

Creating a Band

Lydon was just one of the many British working-class youths who faced an uncertain future that they largely blamed on the conservative economic and social practices of Prime Minister Margaret Thatcher. Thatcher's government, among other things, dismantled many of England's social service agencies and educational services. As a result of England's bleak situation, the country's young people had little to look forward to beyond a life of menial labor or being on "the dole" (welfare).

With few resources, members of this group began to create their own scruffy culture: a fashion statement with an angry political undertone. The style of this subculture featured spiked hair, boots, zippered T-shirts, and jackets that were ripped apart and pinned back together. Headquarters for this "cult with no name" (as one newspaper called it) was a boutique known, at various times, as Sex, Seditionaries, and Too Fast to Live, Too Young to Die.

The shop's owner, Malcolm McLaren, was an aspiring manager who hoped to assemble a band around two teenagers, guitarist Steve Jones and drummer Paul Cook. McLaren recruited a bass player, former shop employee Glen Matlock, and he invented the name the Sex Pistols. But the group still needed a singer, a charismatic front man. Jones and Cook suggested Lydon, whom they had seen hanging around on the street.

Lydon fit the bill perfectly. Because he could not sing, he screamed in a kind of howling chant—but that was fine, because the rest of the group could not play. More importantly than a voice, Cook recalled, Lydon had the right look and attitude: "Bit of a lunatic, [someone] who had definite ideas about what he wanted to do."[91]

New Sensation

The bitter, ironic lyrics for the band's songs were written by Rotten (as he was renamed by his bandmates, allegedly because of his poor dental habits). Songwriting allowed him to make statements about the political and social injustices he saw around him, such as England's royal family, which he regarded as privileged and out of touch. This role as spokesman was to his liking; he later commented, "It suited me fine; all the things I'd wanted to moan about all my measly life I got out in songs."[92]

The band's debut performance was at an art school dance in November 1975. Ten minutes into the gig, horrified by Rotten's scream-

Rotten was chosen as lead singer for the Sex Pistols more for his stage presence than his singing ability.

ing and the deafening volume of his band, the school's social programmer unplugged the amplifiers.

The Pistols managed to find a few other engagements, mostly at art schools and pubs, through the early months of 1976. Wherever they appeared, they caused near riots, thanks largely to Rotten's frantic, snarling stage performance. He incited audiences by spitting on them and insulting them between songs. Audience members reacted by throwing beer cans at the singer or punching each other.

By the summer the jarring music the band played had a name: punk rock. Other bands were beginning to create similar sounds. The press took notice of the punk groundswell. Predictably, politicians and others—including older, more established musicians—condemned the music as a noisy mess. Although the band had not even put a record out, its fame was growing.

At the same time, Rotten solidified his position as the band's public spokesman. He displayed a confident gift for quotable, deliberately outrageous statements. "I don't understand it," he would say in mock surprise about the uproar over the Pistols. "All we're trying to do is destroy everything."[93]

Anarchy

Rotten exploded into national and international celebrity following a now-notorious TV interview late that year. He and the other band members, drunk and bored, were provoked by the show's host into using obscenities on live television. The British public was scandalized, and punk became front-page news instead of just a strange underground cult. In fact, EMI, a high-profile record company, signed the Pistols to a recording contract.

Rotten thrived on the attention, although he also had moments of doubt. One day soon after the notorious TV show, he confessed to his friend Chrissie Hynde (later the leader of the Pretenders) that his growing fame was depressing him. She recalled, "He was afraid his friends would change and that things would change drastically for the worst. He was just a little Irish boy from Finsbury Park. He had really taken on a lot with all this, and I think it freaked him out."[94]

The band was famous, but it had trouble being heard. It could not find gigs, because promoters were fearful of audience violence. After McLaren invented a tale that had the Pistols vomiting and spitting their way through customs at London's Heathrow Airport, nervous EMI executives decided to drop the band. Rotten later commented, "He [McLaren] thought he'd bury us in some kind of mystique and that would help record sales."[95]

Malcolm McLaren (far left) thought that outrageous tales of the band's exploits would help generate record sales.

As a result of the problems with EMI, the band's debut single, "Anarchy in the U.K.," was not released in England. (British fans had to buy French imports.) With its blasting rhythms and virtually incomprehensible vocals, critic Al Spicer notes, "it was everything that punk was supposed to be about."[96]

More Provocative Recordings

The band's reputation for noisy brawling and offensive behavior continued to create controversy and headlines. Its second recording deal, with A&M Records, lasted roughly one week. The Pistols' violent, drunken conduct at the signing party was too much for A&M's nervous executives, who canceled the contract. Manager McLaren garnered excellent publicity from the affair—and kept the advance money from the record company.

During this period Glen Matlock was replaced by Rotten's friend John Ritchie, Rotten's one-time busking partner. Ritchie was renamed Sid Vicious, after Rotten's pet hamster. He could not play the bass but, like Rotten, had the right attitude and look.

A third record company, Virgin, eventually took Rotten and his band on. In 1977, the year of Queen Elizabeth II's Silver Jubilee Celebration, Virgin released a second Pistols single, the deeply cynical "God Save the Queen." To promote the record, the Pistols deliberately provoked Britain's royal family, and Rotten's bitterly antiroyal lyrics scandalized Britain. Citizens' groups picketed the record company. Established rockers like Mick Jagger of the Rolling Stones publicly stated their dislike. No hall in Britain would book the Pistols for a show.

During the controversy, Rotten was the victim of several violent attacks. The worst was when he was stabbed by a man who shouted, "We love the queen." The attack permanently damaged nerves in the singer's arm.

The British Broadcasting Company, the government-owned radio network, banned "God Save the Queen." Nonetheless, the song shot to number one on charts maintained by independent, nonmainstream magazines. On the official record-sales charts, it stayed at the number two position. There, it was "listed" as a blank, because newspaper publishers refused to identify it by name.

In November the band's only album, *Never Mind the Bollocks Here's the Sex Pistols*, was released. The word "bollocks" (British slang for testicles, with a second meaning of "B.S.") was enough to trigger a lawsuit, citing an 1899 law about indecent advertisement. Several large chain stores refused to stock the album, and advertising on TV was banned. Nonetheless, the album went straight to number one.

In a deliberate effort to provoke Britain's royal family, the Sex Pistols sign autographs outside Buckingham Palace prior to the release of "God Save the Queen."

Problems in America

Later that year the band left for an American tour. The journey was a disaster from beginning to end for Rotten. For one thing, he was deeply upset at what he saw as McLaren's manipulative behavior. This included mysterious marketing plans and accounting systems, plus iron-fisted control over finances. Although the Pistols were earning a fortune, each member was on an allowance of sixty pounds each a week—about $100.

In Rotten's opinion, McLaren was an opportunist who ignored problems, tried to turn members of the band against each other, and cheated them blind. "Malcolm wouldn't tell us anything he was up to," Rotten later commented, "so we all felt manipulated and fed up."[97]

Rotten was also incensed at how McLaren was trying to manipulate Rotten's role as front man. McLaren had always envisioned Rotten as a sort of enigmatic poet/spokesman, but the singer had his own ideas. He wanted to speak his own mind, not parrot the ideas of someone behind the scenes. "They wanted me to be this mystery figure they could hide in the cupboard and spring out like a jack-in-the-box," Rotten bitterly remarked. "Close the lid when it's not needed anymore."[98]

A third problem was drug abuse. Vicious had developed a heroin habit so strong that he could barely stand up onstage, much less play. Rotten, always fond of alcohol and amphetamines, was drinking more heavily and taking increasing amounts of speed. The combination helped blank out the chaos around him; it put him, he noted, "up and down—in a deep state of confusion about everything."[99]

Breakup

Another reason the tour was not successful was that it avoided large urban centers like Los Angeles and New York, where Rotten would likely have been well received. Instead, it went to smaller cities in the South and Southwest. Audiences there were unreceptive, and the singer was angrily pelted with food and beer cans at every performance.

By the time the tour reached San Francisco, everything was dissolving. The musicians were not speaking to one another, and Vicious's heroin habit intensified. At the close of a chaotic show in San Francisco, Rotten asked the audience: "Ever have the feeling you've been cheated?"[100]

Many observers assumed the sarcastic comment was meant for the audience. Rotten noted later, however, that it had been aimed elsewhere: "It was directed at us onstage, because we had been cheated, and we cheated ourselves."[101]

After the show the singer announced bitterly to the press that the Sex Pistols were no longer. In the aftermath of the breakup, Jones

After the breakup of the Sex Pistols, Rotten formed a new band, PiL.

and Cook went to Brazil to cut a record with an infamous British train robber in exile. Vicious was indicted for murdering his girlfriend but died of a heroin overdose before going to trial.

Artistically and personally, Rotten fared the best. He took back his original name, Lydon, and initiated a legal battle against McLaren to recover royalties. After several years in the courts, he, Jones, Cook, and Vicious's mother won the suit.

PiL and Beyond

In 1978 Lydon formed a new band, Public Image Ltd. (PiL). The band was a collaboration with guitarist Keith Levene and bassist Jah Wobble (John Wardle) and a changing array of drummers.

In part, the band was formed so that Lydon could mock the crass commercial aspects of the music industry. He called PiL a corporation and insisted it was not a band. Financial adviser Dave Crowe was sometimes credited on albums as a band member.

PiL's sound changed radically from album to album. Its various styles—incorporating thick textures of complex dance rhythms, industrial noise, and world music—were often labeled "antirock."

Many critics commented that the band was a deliberate reaction against the Pistols' ultra-basic, ultra-aggressive crashing rock, just as the Pistols had once reacted against bland superproduced seventies rock.

Lydon disbanded PiL in 1993 but continued as a solo artist. He has since collaborated with a strikingly diverse group of musicians. Among them are rockers Steve Vai, Ryuichi Sakamoto, Ginger Baker, the Golden Palominos, and the Chemical Brothers; world music star L. Shankar; hip-hop legend Afrika Bambaataa; and mainstream soul music artists Tower of Power.

The singer has also ventured into other forms of media. One of these projects was a daily radio show, *Rotten Day*, that offered his acerbic opinions on rock and society.

In 1996 Lydon reunited the Sex Pistols, with Glenn Matlock on bass, for a world tour. Gleefully declaring them "fat, forty and back," Lydon was candid about his intentions in organizing the reunion. He called it the Filthy Lucre [Money] Tour and commented about the band members, "We don't see eye to eye but we have a common interest—your money."[102]

Famous for his bitterness and anger, Rotten has matured in recent years.

Maturity

The singer, originally famous for his bitterness and unrelenting anger, has become almost mellow as he approaches middle age. He is married to Nora Up, a German-born concert promoter, and they maintain homes in Los Angeles, London, and Berlin.

Lydon commented about his maturity, "I've got the same old problems as everybody else. Backaches. Hangover. Gas bills. Two flights of stairs to trundle down until I can have a cup of tea."[103]

Journalist Jeffrey Ressner notes, however, that Lydon "hasn't lost his sarcastic sneer—even if his spiky orange hair and Day-Glo togs make him look more like a Rugrat these days than a rebel."[104]

Lydon has launched several new projects. One is a documentary film about the Sex Pistols, *The Filth and the Fury*. He has also released a PiL compilation album; launched a talk and music show, *Rotten Television*, on the cable TV channel VH1; is an occasional guest on the network television program *Politically Incorrect;* and hosts a four-hour weekly Webcast on the Internet channel eYada.com. Lydon's status as a rock revolutionary, which he earned during his bad-boy youth with the Sex Pistols, ensures his enduring status as a legend. At the same time, he remains a vivid presence on the current cultural scene, a gadfly who points out the weaknesses of life as he sees it.

CHAPTER 8

Kurt Cobain: Reluctant Star

"It was so fast and explosive. I didn't know how to deal with it. If there was a Rock Star 101 course, I would have liked to take it."

—Kurt Cobain

Kurt Cobain brought the sound and spirit of grunge music—the most important development in rock in the 1990s—to mainstream audiences. As leader of the band Nirvana, he was grunge's most visible hero.

Grunge was a style that merged the angry aggressiveness of punk with the hard-edged heavy metal of the 1980s. Heavy metal, unlike punk, emphasized technical ability; the virtuoso guitar solo, for example, was an important element of heavy metal.

When Cobain's fame arrived, it took the singer/songwriter/guitarist by surprise. The struggle with sudden celebrity proved overwhelming for the sensitive and gifted musician, who had always projected an aura of vulnerability and frailty despite the power of his music. Unable to adjust, he committed suicide in 1994 at the age of twenty-seven.

His untimely death cemented his role as a legend of rock. But it was also seen by many as the final wedge driving apart the fragmented rock scene. Where once a handful of stars and a single style had commanded the attention of virtually every rock fan, by the 1990s the audience had split into dozens of audiences, each with its own heroes and heroines.

Because of this increasingly divided audience, some observers feel that Cobain may have been the last great rock legend. Critic Patrick MacDonald of the *Seattle Times* observes, "Things are just too fragmented now. There will never again be a rock star with an appeal as universal as that of Elvis or the Beatles. Not after Kurt."[105]

Aberdeen

Kurt Donald Cobain was born in Hoquiam, Washington, on February 20, 1967, and grew up in nearby Aberdeen. The twin towns are in a harsh, economically depressed logging region on the state's southwest coast. Their bleakness and the way their residents shunned Cobain would later have a profound influence on his songwriting and performance.

Kurt's father, an auto mechanic, and his mother, a part-time secretary, divorced when Kurt was eight. From then until his teens, he lived mostly with his mother but moved frequently among the homes of relatives in the Aberdeen area.

Kurt was sensitive and a natural loner. He felt out of place almost everywhere. One of the few places where he felt welcome was the town library, where he spent many spare hours. "I felt so different and so crazy," he once remarked, "that people just left me alone. They were afraid."[106]

Music was another refuge from his sense of isolation. Kurt grew up loving the Beatles and was thoroughly immersed in their melodic brand of rock. As an adolescent, however, he preferred the harder-edged, more aggressive music of heavy metal bands like Led Zeppelin, Black Sabbath, and Kiss.

Kurt Cobain was a loner who felt out of place wherever he was.

An aunt who noticed Kurt's interest in music gave him a cheap guitar, and he learned by playing along with records. A leftie, he played it upside down. (Later he used guitars made especially for left-handed musicians.)

Kurt found a mentor in Buzz Osborne, a member of a local band called the Melvins. Osborne introduced him to a powerful new kind of music. Kurt was too young to have listened to punk during its heyday of 1976–77, but after he became familiar with it through Osborne, it deeply influenced his own music. He felt that it spoke to his sense of alienation and loneliness, to his sense of being an outsider in society, and to his feelings of frustration over life's uncertainties.

Nirvana Forms

Cobain never finished high school, dropping out just weeks before graduation. He felt increasingly alienated from his peers and school offered him little fulfillment. But he kept persevering with his music, playing in a series of short-lived bands with names like Brown Towel, Ted Ed Fred, and Pen Cap Chew. It was in these bands that he not only honed his singing and playing skills but also began writing songs with ironic and often sarcastic lyrics.

Late in 1986 he formed a trio with a bass player, Chris Novoselic, and a succession of drummers. (Novoselic later changed his name to Krist to reflect his Croatian heritage.) This band was a rudimentary version of Nirvana.

It became clear to Cobain that his time in Aberdeen was at an end if he wanted to pursue music seriously. "Basically," he remarked later about the town, "if you're not prepared to join the logging industry, you're going to be beaten up or run out of town."[107]

He moved to Olympia, the state capital and the home of a liberal arts college. (Novoselic moved to nearby Tacoma.) Olympia was a hotbed of alternative, cutting-edge rock, and Cobain found occasional work playing at parties and clubs. Cobain supported himself there as a janitor and moved in with his first serious girlfriend, Tracy Marander.

Recording and Touring

Cobain quickly earned a reputation as a top performer around Olympia. His music was characterized by a heavy, churning sound, an uninhibited stage performance, and anguished vocals. Word about Cobain eventually reached a small Seattle record label, Sub Pop. Sub Pop was one of the many independent labels that had been inspired by punk's do-it-yourself creed.

The label's owners found Cobain's music compatible with that of other Sub Pop bands, like Mudhoney and Soundgarden. In 1988 and '89, the label released Nirvana's first two singles: "Love Buzz" and "Sliver."

The band's first album, *Bleach*, released in 1989, was an uneven mix of the band's many influences. However, some of Cobain's songs were notable, particularly the melodic "About a Girl" and the superheavy "Blew." Sub Pop was enthusiastic about the record and created a wry promotional campaign for the band: "They're young, they own their own van, and they're going to make us rich!"[108]

Pleased with Cobain's music, the independent record label Sub Pop released Nirvana's first two singles in 1989.

The album was a modest hit in the underground (nonmainstream) rock community. Critics in many fanzines (magazines produced by fans) praised Cobain's budding talents, and college radio stations across the country gave *Bleach* airplay. The album initially sold about thirty-five thousand copies, a respectable figure for an independent-label release.

Following the album's release, Nirvana launched its first tours, traveling across America and Europe by van. A feature of these early shows was the angry destruction of instruments. Since Cobain and the others could hardly afford to buy expensive new equipment, they bought cheap instruments in each town or spent hours repairing existing equipment.

Catching On

The band struggled on in this way with critical success but little wide-spread attention until 1990, which was a watershed year for Cobain.

His health had never been strong, and he suffered from a serious stomach problem that caused intense pain and nausea. It was never properly identified, but the problem may have stemmed from a pinched nerve caused by scoliosis (curvature of the spine) in childhood. In desperation, the guitarist retreated into drugs. Heroin, in common use among Seattle's rock community, had already caused several deaths. Nonetheless, over the winter of 1990, Cobain began using it because, he said, it was the only thing that relieved his suffering.

Nirvana had never found a permanent drummer. Cobain had been searching for one with sufficient power and stamina, personal compatibility, and similar ideas about what he and Novoselic were trying to create musically. During this period, however, Cobain finally found his drummer. Dave Grohl, who had played in the Washington, D.C. band Scream, was a perfect fit. The basic trio of Nirvana was now in place.

Meanwhile, the bands on Sub Pop—who were similar enough to be lumped together in a style called grunge—were beginning to pick up attention. Long the favorites of college alternative rock stations, these bands were finally becoming popular enough in the underground to be noticed by the mainstream music industry. Major record companies began scouring the Pacific Northwest for talent.

Nirvana was considered the most promising of these bands, and a bidding war for its next album was won by the DGC/Geffen label. Signing with a major label was a big step for a band that until recently had been known only to a handful of Northwest rockers. But to music journalist Dawn Anderson, who had followed Cobain since the early days, the deal seemed inevitable, given his charismatic performance and compelling songwriting: "Nobody was surprised they 'got signed.'. . . Nirvana is a grunge band even normal people like."[109]

Nevermind

Cobain's major-label debut, 1991's *Nevermind*, was, in the opinion of many, the most important rock recording of the 1990s. With songs like "Smells Like Teen Spirit," it perfectly captured the frustrated emotions of young people in '90s America.

Nevermind rocketed grunge out of the underground and introduced it to a wide mainstream audience. The album appealed to a broad range of fans thanks to its blend of hard, heavy rock and glossy, pop-oriented production. The album's producer, Butch Vig, emphasized the melodic nature of Cobain's songs. He commented, "Kurt loved the Beatles. He loved John Lennon. So I know that he felt self-conscious, coming from a punk background and having these kind of gorgeously crafted songs. Even though his songs might have been kind of noisy, they still had really beautiful melodies and melodic structure."[110]

Writers Jim Berkenstadt and Charles R. Cross note, "Because it appealed to so many different ages, genders, and nationalities of people, it was one of the few albums of the '90s that found its way into almost

The addition of Dave Grohl (right) in 1990 ended Nirvana's search for a permanent drummer.

every record collection."[111] The record label had predicted modestly healthy sales of a quarter million. To everyone's astonishment, the album streaked past that figure and ultimately sold 10 million copies worldwide. No one was prepared for this. The label's president, Ed Rosenblatt, remarked that the album quickly took on a life of its own: "We didn't do anything. It was just one of those 'get out of the way and duck' records."[112]

The album's freakish success focused attention on other Seattle grunge bands, and other Sub Pop groups became internationally famous almost overnight. Grunge fashion—flannel shirts, sweaters, torn jeans, knit caps—suddenly became an ultra-hip style featured in the pages of the normally staid *New York Times*. And Kurt Cobain went from scruffy musician/janitor to superstar.

Because of Nirvana's national exposure, the grunge look became a popular fashion trend.

Pressure

He never felt comfortable in that role, however. Krist Novoselic later commented that the guitarist would have been satisfied playing in small clubs: "As long as he could make enough to put gas in the car and buy strings for his guitar, he was content."[113]

Cobain hated the sudden attention on his every move and statement. He thought the focus on him made him seem phony and arrogant. The very fact that his music was loved by millions offended him. He worried that his new fans were not listening carefully to the songs and were missing the points of his messages.

Cobain reacted by becoming as obnoxious as possible in public. He made provocative and offensive statements onstage and in interviews, destroyed his equipment before sets were finished, or walked offstage in midset. "I found myself being overly obnoxious," he recalled, "because I noticed that there were more average people coming into our shows and I didn't want them there. They started to get on my nerves."[114]

Meanwhile, the singer was experiencing the common anxieties of celebrity: he was frightened of being attacked or becoming isolated. He hinted that the pressure might not be worth keeping Nirvana alive: "I still love to be in a band and play music with Chris and Dave, but if it means that we have to resort to playing in a practice room and never touring again, then so be it."[115]

As the pressure increased, Cobain's heroin use became more frequent and heavy, his behavior increasingly erratic. Always moody, the singer now swung rapidly between emotional highs and lows. Writer Jon Pareles noted that during an interview Cobain "ricochets between opposites. He is wary and unguarded, sincere and sarcastic, thin-skinned and insensitive, aware of his popularity and trying to ignore it."[116]

Family

While in Los Angeles recording *Nevermind*, Cobain had struck up a romance with Courtney Love, the flamboyant leader of the band Hole. Married in Hawaii on February 24, 1992, the couple briefly lived in Los Angeles before buying a waterfront house in Seattle.

The next year Love gave birth to a girl, Frances Bean Cobain. Because Love had admitted to using heroin in the early stages of the pregnancy,

Pictured with Cobain are his wife Courtney Love and their daughter Frances Bean Cobain.

the Children's Services Department of Los Angeles County (where the baby had been born) immediately challenged the couple's fitness to be parents. Their baby was briefly taken from them. Even after Cobain and Love regained custody of Frances, authorities did not trust their abilities as parents. The baby's rearing was supervised until the spring of 1993.

Cobain seemed delighted with his new roles of father and husband, but a series of events in the spring and summer of 1993 indicated that he was on a personal downward spiral. In May emergency services were called when he overdosed on heroin at his Seattle home. The next month police were summoned there again following a noisy argument between Cobain and Love over Cobain's gun collection. They confiscated some of the singer's guns and some pills, but no charges were filed. Then, in July, in a New York hotel room before a show, Cobain overdosed again.

New Directions

Meanwhile, Cobain kept working. There were several indications that he was searching for new directions. His next studio album, *In Utero*, was a marked departure from the glossy *Nevermind*. The guitarist and his producer deliberately buried Cobain's melodies, which were often very beautiful, under a ragged, thick wall of sound. Record label executives worried about this lack of polish and about the album's provocative cover art, but *In Utero* debuted at number one.

Another direction Cobain pursued was the inclusion of an acoustic set in concert, and a third was a change in the band's lineup. For a European tour early in 1994, Cobain added a rhythm guitarist, Pat Smear, and a cellist, Lori Goldstein, to the band. Smear had been a member of the L.A. punk band the Germs, and Goldstein played with a Seattle band, the Black Cat Orchestra.

All these changes reflected ideas Cobain had been openly expressing in interviews: his boredom with the trio format and his eagerness to expand his musical horizons. "We're almost exhausted," Cobain told a reporter regarding the band's basic setup. "We've gone to the point where things are becoming repetitious."[117]

Unfortunately, Cobain's attempts at forging a new direction were short-lived. Because of the guitarist's fragile condition, the European tour was canceled after only a handful of shows. Cobain and Love remained in Rome. Early on the morning of March 4, Love found her husband unconscious in their hotel bathroom, overdosed on a combination of alcohol and Rohypnol, a powerful tranquilizer.

Cobain remained in a coma for twenty hours in a Roman hospital before becoming well enough to return to Seattle. At first the in-

Cobain's suicide note indicated burnout and a desire to quit music as reasons for killing himself.

cident was deemed an accident, but later the existence of a suicide note was revealed.

The End

Matters did not improve at home. On March 18 police were summoned to Cobain's house, where the singer had locked himself in a room with a gun and was threatening to kill himself. The police managed to talk him into surrendering the gun.

At the end of March, Cobain checked into a drug and alcohol detoxification clinic in Los Angeles. However, he fled on April 1, scaling a wall after telling staff that he was going outside for a cigarette.

A missing persons report was filed, and Love hired a private detective. Cobain's whereabouts remained a mystery until April 8, when an electrician hired to fit the Seattle house with a new security system found the guitarist in a room above the garage. He was dead, of a self-inflicted shotgun wound to the head, at the age of twenty-seven.

Next to his body, police found a box containing burnt spoons, needles, and other drug paraphernalia. An autopsy later revealed a high concentration of heroin and traces of other drugs in Cobain's system.

Police also found a long, rambling note next to the body. Most of it seemed merely to indicate Cobain's feeling of burnout and his desire to quit the music business. "I haven't felt the excitement of listening to, as well as creating music for too many years now," the note read in part. "I feel guilty beyond words about those things."[118]

After His Death

An atmosphere of shocked disbelief followed the announcement of the singer's death. Mourners staged a vigil around a fountain at Seattle Center, listening to Cobain's music, lighting candles, and singing.

Cobain's mother summed up the feelings of many in a poignant statement to the press. Referring to the price many rock stars have paid for stardom, she told a reporter, "Now he's gone and joined that stupid club. I told him not to join that stupid club."[119]

For weeks afterward the media talked about Cobain and the generation he had represented. On the Internet and elsewhere, there was intense speculation questioning the official ruling of suicide. A number of theories speculated, sometimes wildly, that Cobain was murdered.

The media and others also analyzed and dissected the intense pressure of stardom, especially on those unprepared for it. Typical was a piece by journalist David Fricke, who writes, "In blind desperation, immune even to his own native instincts, Kurt Cobain violently and deliberately ended his own life. If you really want to be cold about it, he abruptly altered the course of rock by removing himself from the gameboard. The stakes had gotten too high, the options too complicated, the rewards too suffocating."[120]

Ironically, the act of "removing himself from the gameboard" has assured Cobain's continuing status as rock legend. The performer hated fame and everything that came with it, and suicide was apparently the only solution he saw to his problems. However, in large part as a result of his dramatic and untimely end, Cobain's meteoric career and music will remain imprinted in the public's mind. Cobain, like the other rock legends in this book, remains a major figure in rock music's ongoing story. Each legend represents a pivotal point in rock's evolution and growth, and each is an important influence for the musicians of today and tomorrow.

NOTES

Introduction: Testing the Boundaries

1. Dave Marsh, *Glory Days: The Bruce Springsteen Story, Volume II*. New York: Thunder's Mouth Press, 1996, p. 34.
2. Quoted in Eric Alterman, *It Ain't No Sin to Be Glad You're Alive: The Promise of Bruce Springsteen*. Boston: Little, Brown, 1999, p. 171.

Chapter 1: A Brief History of Rock

3. Author interview with Sonny Bono, 1988.
4. Robert Palmer, *Rock and Roll: An Unruly History*. New York: Harmony Books, 1995, p. 76.
5. Ed Ward, Geoffrey Stokes, and Ken Tucker, *Rock of Ages: The Rolling Stone History of Rock & Roll*. New York: Rolling Stone Press, 1986, p. 377.
6. Quoted in Timothy White, *Rock Lives*. New York: Henry Holt, 1990, p. 269.
7. Mikal Gilmore, *Night Beat*. New York: Doubleday, 1998, p. 56.
8. Patrick MacDonald, "Morrison and Mitchell: As Good as It Gets," *Seattle Times*, May 14, 1998, p. G5.
9. Marsh, *Glory Days*, pp. 35–36.
10. Quoted in Scott Schinder, ed., *Rolling Stone's Alt-Rock-a-Rama*. New York: Dell, 1996, p. 34.
11. Quoted in Roger Sabin, ed., *Punk Rock: So What?: The Cultural Legacy of Punk*. London: Routledge, 1999, p. 53.

Chapter 2: Elvis Presley: The King of Rock and Roll

12. Quoted in Jerry Hopkins, *Elvis*. New York: Simon & Schuster, 1971, p. 22.
13. Quoted in Dave Marsh, *Elvis*. New York: Thunder's Mouth Press, 1992, p. 9.
14. Quoted in Marsh, *Elvis*, p. 21.
15. Quoted in Hopkins, *Elvis*, p. 65.
16. Quoted in Peter Guralnick, *Last Train to Memphis: The Rise of Elvis Presley*. Boston: Little, Brown, 1994, p. 92.

17. Quoted in Guralnick, *Last Train to Memphis*, p. 92.

18. Quoted in Howard A. DeWitt, *Elvis: The Sun Years*. Ann Arbor: Popular Culture, 1993, p. 154.

19. Quoted in Guralnick, *Last Train to Memphis*, p. 474.

20. Quoted in Hopkins, *Elvis*, p. 376.

21. Quoted in Jerry Hopkins, *Elvis: The Final Years*. New York: St. Martin's Press, 1980, p. 138.

22. Quoted in Steve Dunleavy with Red West, Sonny West, and Dave Hebler, *Elvis: What Happened?* New York: Ballantine Books, 1977, p. 202.

23. Quoted in Hopkins, *Elvis: The Final Years*, p. 239.

24. Quoted in Hopkins, *Elvis: The Final Years*, p. 245.

Chapter 3: John Lennon: Working-class Hero

25. Quoted in Hunter Davies, *The Beatles*. New York: McGraw-Hill, 1978, p. 13.

26. Quoted in Philip Norman, *Shout!* New York: Simon & Schuster, 1981, p. 34.

27. Quoted in Mark Hertsgaard, *A Day in the Life*. New York: Delacorte, 1995, p. 113.

28. Quoted in Gareth L. Pawlowki, *How They Became the Beatles*. New York: Dutton, 1989, p. 156.

29. Quoted in Norman, *Shout!*, p. 214.

30. Quoted in Brian Epstein, *A Cellarful of Noise*. Ann Arbor: Pierian Press, 1984, p. 100.

31. Quoted in Nicholas Schaffner, *The Beatles Forever*. Harrisburg, PA: Stackpole Books, 1977, p. 57.

32. Quoted in Jann Wenner, *Lennon Remembers*. San Francisco: Straight Arrow Books, 1971, p. 56.

33. Quoted in Ray Coleman, *Lennon: The Definitive Biography*. New York: HarperPerennial, 1992, p. 529.

34. Quoted in Geoffrey Stokes, *The Beatles*. New York: Rolling Stone Press, 1980, p. 222.

35. Quoted in Norman, *Shout!*, p. 366.

36. Quoted in Schaffner, *The Beatles Forever*, p. 138.

37. Quoted in Hertsgaard, *A Day in the Life*, p. 244.

38. Quoted in Coleman, *Lennon*, p. 591.

39. Quoted in Coleman, *Lennon*, p. 680.

40. Quoted in Alterman, *It Ain't No Sin to be Glad You're Alive*, p. 124.

Chapter 4: Janis Joplin: Full-Tilt Boogie

41. Myra Friedman, *Buried Alive: The Biography of Janis Joplin*. New York: Harmony, 1983, pp. xiii–xiv.

42. Quoted in Alice Echols, *Scars of Sweet Paradise: The Life and Times of Janis Joplin*, New York: Metropolitan Books, 1999, p. 35.

43. Echols, *Scars of Sweet Paradise*, p. 26.

44. Quoted in Ellis Amburn, *Pearl: The Obsessions and Passions of Janis Joplin*. New York: Warner Books, 1992, p. 21.

45. Quoted in Amburn, *Pearl*, p. 22.

46. Quoted in Echols, *Scars of Sweet Paradise*, p. 75.

47. Quoted in Friedman, *Buried Alive*, p. 74.

48. Quoted in Echols, *Scars of Sweet Paradise,* p. 132.

49. Quoted in Amburn, *Pearl*, p. 77.

50. Friedman, *Buried Alive*, p. 86.

51. Quoted in Jonathan Buckley and Mark Ellingham, eds., *Rock: The Rough Guide*. London: Rough Guide Press, 1996, p. 467.

52. Quoted in Echols, *Scars of Sweet Paradise*, p. 215.

53. Quoted in Laura Joplin, *Love, Janis*. New York: Villard Books, 1992, p. 244.

54. Quoted in Friedman, *Buried Alive*, p. 161.

55. Quoted in Friedman, *Buried Alive*, p. 335.

56. David Henderson, *'Scuse Me While I Kiss the Sky: The Life of Jimi Hendrix*. New York: Bantam, 1996, p. 211.

57. Quoted in Echols, *Scars of Sweet Paradise*, p. 224.

Chapter 5: Jimi Hendrix: Guitar Warrior-Poet

58. Quoted in Henderson, *'Scuse Me While I Kiss the Sky*, p. 227.

59. Charles Shaar Murray, *Crosstown Traffic: Jimi Hendrix and the Post-War Rock 'n' Roll Revolution*. New York: St. Martin's, 1989, p. 34.

60. Harry Shapiro and Caesar Glebbeek, *Jimi Hendrix: Electric Gypsy*. New York: St. Martin's, 1990, p. 25.

61. Quoted in Henderson, *'Scuse Me While I Kiss the Sky*, p. 24.

62. Quoted in Shapiro and Glebbeek, *Jimi Hendrix*, p. 41.

63. Quoted in Shapiro and Glebbeek, *Jimi Hendrix*, p. 69.

64. Henderson, *'Scuse Me While I Kiss the Sky*, p. 54.

65. Quoted in Anthony DeCurtis and James Heinke, eds., *The Rolling Stone Illustrated History of Rock & Roll*. New York: Rolling Stone Press, 1992, p. 298.

66. Quoted in Paul Friedlander, *Rock and Roll: A Social History*. New York: HarperCollins, 1996, p. 224.

67. Quoted in Shapiro and Glebbeek, *Jimi Hendrix*, p. 275.

68. Murray, *Crosstown Traffic*, p. 54.

69. Quoted in DeCurtis and Heinke, *The Rolling Stone Illustrated History of Rock & Roll*, p. 302.

70. Quoted in Jerry Hopkins, *Hit and Run: The Jimi Hendrix Story*. New York: Putnam, 1983, p. 304.

71. Quoted in Shapiro and Glebbeek, *Jimi Hendrix*, p. 401.

Chapter 6: Bruce Springsteen: The Boss

72. Quoted in Alterman, *It Ain't No Sin to Be Glad You're Alive*, p. 272.

73. Quoted in Marsh, *Glory Days*, p. 75.

74. Quoted in Alterman, *It Ain't No Sin to Be Glad You're Alive*, p. 17.

75. Quoted in Dave Marsh, *Born to Run: The Bruce Springsteen Story, Volume I*. New York: Thunder's Mouth Press, 1996, p. 28.

76. Quoted in Alterman, *It Ain't No Sin to Be Glad You're Alive*, p. 11.

77. Quoted in Alterman, *It Ain't No Sin to be Glad You're Alive*, p. 25.

78. Quoted in DeCurtis and Heinke, *The Rolling Stone Illustrated History of Rock & Roll*, p. 620.

79. Quoted in Marsh, *Born to Run*, p. 118.

80. Quoted in Editors of *Rolling Stone*, *Bruce Springsteen: The Rolling Stone Files*. New York: Hyperion, 1996, p. 14.

81. Quoted in Buckley and Ellingham, *Rock: The Rough Guide*, p. 831.

82. Quoted in Alterman, *It Ain't No Sin to Be Glad You're Alive*, p. 148.

83. Quoted in Editors of *Rolling Stone*, *Bruce Springsteen*, p. 21.

84. Quoted in Alterman, *It Ain't No Sin to Be Glad You're Alive*, p. 159.

85. Eric Alterman, "Rock & Roll Fantasies (Bruce Springsteen's Song 'American Skin' Draws Complaints)," *Nation*, July 17, 2000, p. 12.

86. Quoted in Editors of *Rolling Stone*, *Bruce Springsteen*, p. 22.

87. Marsh, *Glory Days*, p. xxx.

88. Quoted in Alterman, *It Ain't No Sin to Be Glad You're Alive*, p. 204.

89. Quoted in Editors of *Rolling Stone*, *Bruce Springsteen*, p. 321

Chapter Seven: Johnny Rotten: King of Punk

90. John Lydon, *Rotten: No Irish, No Blacks, No Dogs*. New York: St. Martin's Press, 1994, p. 66.

91. Quoted in DeCurtis and Heinke, *The Rolling Stone Illustrated History of Rock & Roll*, p. 451.

92. Quoted in Adrian Boot and Chris Salewicz, *Punk: The Illustrated History of a Music Revolution*. New York: Penguin, 1996, p. 104.

93. Quoted in DeCurtis and Heinke, *The Rolling Stone Illustrated History of Rock & Roll*, p. 455.

94. Lydon, *Rotten*, p. 137

95. Quoted in Boot and Salewicz, *Punk*, p. 99.

96. Quoted in Buckley and Ellingham, *Rock*, p. 770.

97. Lydon, *Rotten*, p. 250.

98. Quoted in David Dalton, *El Sid: Saint Vicious*. New York: St. Martin's Press, 1997, pp. 76–77.

99. Lydon, *Rotten*, p. 99.

100. Quoted in Schinder, *Rolling Stone's Alt-Rock-a-Rama*, p. 299.

101. Quoted in Palmer, *Rock and Roll*, p. 278.

102. Quoted in Belinda Luscombe, "Seen & Heard," *Time*, April 1, 1996, p. 85.

103. Quoted in Daniel Rosenberg, "Questions for John Lydon: Johnny Goes to Hollywood," *New York Times*, March 12, 2000, p. 27.

104. Jeffrey Ressner, "A Rotten Good Time," *Time*, April 17, 2000, p. 81.

Chapter 8: Kurt Cobain: Reluctant Star

105. In private conversation with the author, August 16, 2000.

106. Quoted in Martin Clarke and Paul Woods, eds., *Kurt Cobain: The Cobain Dossier*. London: Plexus, 1999, p. 150.

107. Quoted in Jim Berkenstadt and Charles R. Cross, *Nevermind: Nirvana*. New York: Schirmer, 1998, p. 15.

108. Quoted in Berkenstadt and Cross, *Nevermind*, p. 22.

109. Quoted in John Rocco, ed., *The Nirvana Companion: Two Decades of Commentary*. New York: Schirmer, 1998, p. 15.

110. Quoted in Berkenstadt and Cross, *Nevermind*, p. 63.

111. Berkenstadt and Cross, *Nevermind*, p. 134.

112. Quoted in Michael Azerrad, *Come as You Are: The Story of Nirvana*. New York: Doubleday, 1993, p. 228.

113. Quoted in Berkenstadt and Cross, *Nevermind*, p. 111.

114. Quoted in Azerrad, *Come as You Are*, p. 200.

115. Quoted in Rocco, *The Nirvana Companion*, p. 77.

116. Quoted in Rocco, *The Nirvana Companion*, p. 155.

117. Quoted in Editors of *Rolling Stone, Cobain*. New York: Rolling Stone Press, 1994, p. 69.

118. Quoted in Clarke and Woods, *Kurt Cobain*, p. 7.

119. Quoted in Editors of *Rolling Stone, Cobain*, p. 90.

120. Quoted in Rocco, *The Nirvana Companion*, p. 235.

Chuck Crisafulli, *Teen Spirit: The Stories Behind Every Nirvana Song*. New York: Fireside, 1996. Not written specifically for young adults, but a well-illustrated and detailed look at Kurt Cobain's music.

Ron Frankl, *Bruce Springsteen*. Philadelphia: Chelsea House, 1994. A well-written biography for young readers.

Peter Goddard, *Springsteen Live*. New York: Beaufort Books, 1984. Minimal text but plenty of concert shots of the singer.

Andrew Gracie, *Kurt Cobain*. Philadelphia: Chelsea House, 1998. Part of a series called They Died Too Young, this brief biography has no footnotes or attributions.

Elianne Halbersberg, *Bruce Springsteen*. Cresskill, NJ: Sharon, 1984. A large, heavily illustrated book about the Boss.

Sean Piccoli, *Jimi Hendrix*. Philadelphia: Chelsea House, 1997. A biography for young readers, well illustrated but lacks footnotes and attributions.

David Shirley, *The History of Rock and Roll*. New York: Franklin Watts, 1995. A concise and well-written book for young adults, although it spends little time on rock's black influences and offshoots.

Pete Shotton and Nicholas Schaffner, *John Lennon: In My Life*. New York: Stein and Day, 1983. A memoir by Lennon's lifelong friend Pete Shotton.

Tom Stockdale, *Jimi Hendrix*. Philadelphia: Chelsea House, 1998. A brief biography about Jimi Hendrix for young readers.

———, *John Lennon*. Philadelphia: Chelsea House, 1998. A brief biography about John Lennon for young readers.

David K. Wright, *John Lennon: The Beatles and Beyond*. Springfield, NJ: Enslow Publishers, 1996. A brief biography for young readers about the life and music of John Lennon.

WORKS CONSULTED

Books

Eric Alterman, *It Ain't No Sin to Be Glad You're Alive: The Promise of Bruce Springsteen*. Boston: Little, Brown, 1999. Relying heavily on previously published material, this book attempts to place Springsteen in a sociopolitical context.

Ellis Amburn, *Pearl: The Obsessions and Passions of Janis Joplin*. New York: Warner Books, 1992. Written by a specialist in sensationalist celebrity biographies, this book has some useful quotations nonetheless.

Michael Azerrad, *Come as You Are: The Story of Nirvana*. New York: Doubleday, 1993. An authorized biography of the band, by a *Rolling Stone* writer.

Jim Berkenstadt and Charles R. Cross, *Nevermind: Nirvana*. New York: Schirmer, 1998. Part of the Classic Rock Albums series detailing breakthrough recordings.

Adrian Boot and Chris Salewicz, *Punk: The Illustrated History of a Music Revolution*. New York: Penguin, 1996. Great photos and minimal text by a British writer-photographer team who were closely involved in the punk movement.

Jonathan Buckley and Mark Ellingham, eds., *Rock: The Rough Guide*. London: Rough Guide Press, 1996. This encyclopedia is opinionated and lively.

Martin Clarke and Paul Woods, eds., *Kurt Cobain: The Cobain Dossier*. London: Plexus, 1999. A collection of pieces by British journalists.

Ray Coleman, *Lennon: The Definitive Biography*. New York: Harper-Perennial, 1992. An updated edition of British journalist Coleman's exhaustive, well-written 1985 book.

Charles R. Cross, ed., *Backstreets: Springsteen: The Man and His Music*. New York: Harmony, 1989. Essays by contributors to *Backstreets*, the most prominent fanzine about the Boss.

David Dalton, *El Sid: Saint Vicious*. New York: St. Martin's Press, 1997. A brief rendering of the late Sex Pistol's life.

Hunter Davies, *The Beatles*. New York: McGraw-Hill, 1978. A revised edition of the authorized biography. Heavily censored but basically factual. Originally written in 1968, with a short chapter added to bring its history up to 1978.

Anthony DeCurtis and James Heinke, eds., *The Rolling Stone Illustrated History of Rock & Roll*. New York: Rolling Stone Press, 1992. Probably the single best source of information and photos on rock, this is the revised edition of a book published in 1980.

Howard A. DeWitt, *Elvis: The Sun Years*. Ann Arbor: Popular Culture, 1993. A detailed history and musical analysis of Elvis Presley's early recording years.

Steve Dunleavy with Red West, Sonny West, and Dave Hebler, *Elvis: What Happened?* New York: Ballantine Books, 1977. A tell-all book by three disgruntled ex-Presley employees and ghostwriter Dunleavy.

Alice Echols, *Scars of Sweet Paradise: The Life and Times of Janis Joplin*. New York: Metropolitan Books, 1999. Far and away the best and most evenhanded of the Joplin biographies.

Editors of *Rolling Stone, Bruce Springsteen: The Rolling Stone Files*. New York: Hyperion, 1996. A chronological compendium of writings about Springsteen from the pages of *Rolling Stone* magazine.

———, *Cobain*. New York: Rolling Stone Press, 1994. A well-organized collection of pieces about the late Cobain.

Brian Epstein, *A Cellarfull of Noise*. Ann Arbor: Pierian Press, 1984. The memoir of the manager who brought the Beatles to international fame.

Chet Flippo, *Yesterday*. New York: Doubleday, 1988. An unauthorized biography of Paul McCartney by a veteran rock writer.

Paul Friedlander, *Rock and Roll: A Social History*. New York: HarperCollins, 1996. This concise history by a musician and professor of popular music is designed for use as a college textbook.

Myra Friedman, *Buried Alive: The Biography of Janis Joplin*. New York: Harmony, 1983. A revised edition of a biography originally published in 1973, written by a friend and colleague of the singer.

Mikal Gilmore, *Night Beat*. New York: Doubleday, 1998. A book of incisive and highly readable essays, reviews, and interviews by a veteran writer for *Rolling Stone* and other publications.

Geoffrey Guiliano, ed., *The Lost Beatles Interviews*. New York: Dutton, 1994. A misleadingly titled book, padded with kiss-and-tell junk but with a few good sections.

Peter Guralnick, *Last Train to Memphis: The Rise of Elvis Presley*. Boston: Little, Brown, 1994. The first volume of the best books ever written about Elvis Presley. Wide-ranging, detailed, respectful, and perceptive.

David Henderson, *'Scuse Me While I Kiss the Sky: The Life of Jimi Hendrix*. New York: Bantam, 1996. An updated reissue of an unorthodox biography of the musician, originally published in 1978.

Mark Hertsgaard, *A Day in the Life*. New York: Delacorte, 1995. A well-written, easily readable, extensively researched book that focuses on the music recorded by the Beatles.

Robert Hilburn, *Springsteen*. New York: Rolling Stone Press, 1985. A thoughtful essay by the rock critic for the *Los Angeles Times,* with excellent historical photos.

Jerry Hopkins, *Elvis*. New York: Simon & Schuster, 1971. A dull but straightforward biography that covers the basic facts of Elvis's life through the late 1960s.

———, *Elvis: The Final Years*. New York: St. Martin's Press, 1980. A sequel to the above book, covering Presley's last years. Marred (as is the earlier book) by a lack of citations and index.

———, *Hit and Run: The Jimi Hendrix Story*. New York: Putnam, 1983. A somewhat dry but competent biography about the life of Jimi Hendrix.

Patrick Humphries and Chris Hunt, *Bruce Springsteen: Blinded by the Light*. New York: Henry Holt, 1985. A large-format book about the Boss.

Laura Joplin, *Love, Janis*. New York: Villard Books, 1992. A memoir by the singer's younger sister.

Kurt Loder, *Bat Chain Puller*. New York: St. Martin's Press, 1990. An excellent collection of essays and interviews by a longtime rock critic, this book focuses on the ways rock music and celebrity interact.

John Lydon, *Rotten: No Irish, No Blacks, No Dogs*. New York: St. Martin's Press, 1994. This "unauthorized" autobiography, cowritten with Keith and Kent Zimmerman, is colorful but self-serving.

Dave Marsh, *Born to Run: The Bruce Springsteen Story, Volume I*. New York: Thunder's Mouth Press, 1996. A reissue of the first part of the definitive biography, by a prominent rock critic.

———, *Elvis*. New York: Thunder's Mouth Press, 1992. An intelligent, fair, and passionate book. Not a full biography, but an extended essay with excellent graphics.

———, *Glory Days: The Bruce Springsteen Story, Volume II*. New York: Thunder's Mouth Press, 1996. The second part of Marsh's work.

George Martin, *With a Little Help from My Friends*. Boston: Little, Brown, 1994. A detailed look at the making of the groundbreaking *Sgt. Pepper* album.

Legs McNeil and Gillian McClain, *Please Kill Me: The Uncensored Oral History of Punk*. New York: Grove Press, 1996. McNeil, as editor of a seminal punk fanzine and an eyewitness to the movement, recounts the rise of punk music. The book includes personal accounts from musicians, fans, and others who were part of the scene.

Charles Shaar Murray, *Crosstown Traffic: Jimi Hendrix and the Post-War Rock 'n' Roll Revolution.* New York: St. Martin's, 1989. A thoughtful book about the musician and his musical roots, by a prominent British rock journalist.

Philip Norman, *Shout!* New York: Simon & Schuster, 1981. Probably the best single-volume biography/history of the Beatles, because of its thoroughness, even-handedness, and perceptive insights.

Robert Palmer, *Rock and Roll: An Unruly History.* New York: Harmony Books, 1995. Not a straightforward history but essential reading for anyone interested in the subject, this book was written by one of America's most distinguished writers on popular music. It accompanies the fascinating ten-hour PBS series *Rock and Roll.*

Gareth L. Pawlowki, *How They Became the Beatles.* New York: Dutton, 1989. An obsessively detailed history of the Beatles' early years. Full of wonderful early newspaper clippings, photos, and posters.

John Rocco, ed., *The Nirvana Companion: Two Decades of Commentary.* New York: Schirmer, 1998. A nicely assembled collection of pieces, edited by a university professor.

Roger Sabin, ed., *Punk Rock: So What?: The Cultural Legacy of Punk.* London: Routledge, 1999. A collection of scholarly essays edited by a British academician.

Nicholas Schaffner, *The Beatles Forever.* Harrisburg, PA: Stackpole Books, 1977. A scrapbook-style collection of memorabilia and anecdotes that focus on the impact the Beatles made on pop culture.

Scott Schinder, ed., *Rolling Stone's Alt-Rock-a-Rama.* New York: Dell, 1996. A funny and irreverent look at many aspects of the alternative music scene, which is broadly defined here to include many aspects of modern rock.

Harry Shapiro and Caesar Glebbeek, *Jimi Hendrix: Electric Gypsy.* New York: St. Martin's, 1990. A massive, clearly written, and very thorough biography with many excellent photos of Hendrix as a youth.

Geoffrey Stokes, *The Beatles.* New York: Rolling Stone Press, 1980. A large and lavishly illustrated critical biography by a veteran *Rolling Stone* writer.

Ed Ward, Geoffrey Stokes, and Ken Tucker, *Rock of Ages: The Rolling Stone History of Rock & Roll.* New York: Rolling Stone Press,

1986. This extremely detailed study is an adjunct to the Illustrated History series of essays also published by *Rolling Stone* magazine.

Jann Wenner, *Lennon Remembers*. San Francisco: Straight Arrow Books, 1971. A compilation of two interviews done in late 1970 and early 1971 by *Rolling Stone*'s founder and editor.

Timothy White, *Rock Lives*. New York: Henry Holt, 1990. A massive volume of profiles and interviews by a veteran rock historian, this is full of fascinating information but is also sometimes long-winded.

Periodicals

Eric Alterman, "Rock & Roll Fantasies (Bruce Springsteen's Song 'American Skin' Draws Complaints)," *The Nation*, July 17, 2000, p. 12.

Jeff Giles, "Reborn to Run, Again and Again: Springsteen and His Band Reunite," *Newsweek*, August 2, 1999, p.63.

Belinda Luscombe, "Seen & Heard," *Time*, April 1, 1996, p. 85.

Patrick MacDonald, "Morrison and Mitchell: As Good as It Gets," *Seattle Times*, May 14, 1998.

Jeffrey Ressner, "A Rotten Good Time," *Time*, April 17, 2000, p. 81.

Daniel Rosenberg, "Questions for John Lydon: Johnny Goes to Hollywood," *New York Times*, March 12, 2000, p. 27.

INDEX

PICTURE CREDITS

ABOUT THE AUTHOR

Adam Woog has written over two dozen books, including, for Lucent, biographies of Elvis Presley and the Beatles. He also edited and contributed to *Crossroads*, a book about the Experience Music Project in Seattle, Washington. Woog lives with his wife and daughter in his hometown of Seattle.